To my family, my friends, and colleagues who have stood with me through all the chapters of my life. Without you, I would not be the whole of the sum of my parts and not have ventured to *Growth Without The Bullsh*t*. I offer my most sincere and enduring love, for your spirit, for your support.

Malcom C. McCullough

GROWTH

WITHOUT

THE BULLSH*T

A Grounded Guide To

Change That Works

In Real Life

Malcom C. McCullough

Disclaimer

This Guide provides general information only. It is not medical, psychological, legal, or financial advice. Always seek guidance from a qualified professional. Results vary and are not guaranteed.

Limit of liability

Privacy

Some names and identifying details have been changed or combined. This is an original work reinterpreted through a contemporary framework.

First edition: January 2026
Published by Cherub Publishing Australia
ISBN: 978-1-7642999-5-4

For permissions or inquiries, contact the publisher.

Cherub Publishing Australia

Post Office Box: 1775

Cairns, 4870

FNQ, Queensland, Australia.

About The Author

Malcom C. McCullough (Mal) lives in Cairns, Far North Queensland, Australia. He brings to his writing a wealth of personal and professional experiences, as well as decades of service in the not-for-profit sector. With a distinctive voice shaped by both his own hardship of loss, redemption and hope, he writes about personal change for people who are tired of hype and ready for something more realistic and believes *Growth* should make life steadier, not louder.

He has had a highly diverse career history including, in a range of Government and Community Services, including Infantry Soldier, Police Officer, and managing Youth Services, Homeless Accommodation Services, Drug and Alcohol Accommodation Service. Before his retirement he was an Executive Officer caring for Veterans' and their families. He has experienced, firsthand, the wide ranging personal, family and community impacts that individuals and families endure in the face of loss, pain and trauma.

With decades of experience in leadership, community service, and supporting people through real-world challenges, his work focuses on practical *Growth* that holds up under pressure. His writing rejects quick fixes and empty motivation in favour of grounded insight, clear thinking, and change that works in everyday life.

A Fellow the Goulburn Valley Community Leadership Program and Fellow of the Institute of Community Directors Australia. He has studied and attained, *Advanced Diploma of Community Service Management, Diploma Neuroscience of Leadership, Diploma Community Development, Diploma Community Services, Diploma Business (Governance).*

Contents

Three Ways To Use This Guide

THIS GUIDE IS DESIGNED TO SIT IN THE *REAL LIFE,* not the *lab coat* section of your bookshelf, as it's here to be useful not to win points in an academic arm-wrestle. I lean on work from psychiatry, psychology, neuroscience and trauma research, especially people like David Rock, Dan Siegel, Norman Doidge, and Journalist Lisa Feldman Barrett. They've spent decades in clinics, labs and classrooms, and their ideas have filtered into what you're reading now.

Within these pages, key ideas resurface repeatedly. That's not a glitch, it's training. Every time a concept comes back around, your brain strengthens the path to it, think of it like cutting a track through long grass, one pass helps, ten passes make a trail, with a hundred passes, you can walk it in the dark. That's *Neuroplasticity* at work, the brain changing itself with use. It's how you learnt to walk, ride a bike, drive a car, cook your favourite meal. Not from one magical lesson but from honest repetition until the awkward becomes fluent. Sociologist Anthony Giddens stated, *"Almost every activity that an individual easily performs now was at some time something that required serious mobilization of effort."*

How about reading and absorbing the concepts chapter by chapter, a week at a time. Read the chapter, take notes, re-read, let it all sink in, set some plans, re-read, undertake the early stages of *Growth* and then when you believe you're ready, on to the next chapter. I want you to remember, you didn't get to where you are now in only 34 Weeks, it most likely took you years! So don't see this journey as a magic bullet, see it as a stepped plan, over 34 weeks to lay down the basics. It's worth noting that a Human can be created and born anew in near enough the same time, so there is a precedent!

The idea is that you can move on through the chapters in sequence or you can jump in and out of order according to your need, remember this is your journey, if you want to rush through, go ahead, if you want to savour each chapter week by week, if you want to start at the end, do that as well, whatever you choose is your decision.

Let's make a plan. I don't, wouldn't, expect you to absorb, remember, practice every concept or idea in the following pages, so I am thinking that we can agree that we treat *Growth Without The Bullsh*t*, to be eaten like an elephant, piece by piece, small manageable chucks. I really don't want you to overload and start chocking and eventually throwing the Guide to the *Sh*t House.*

You'll notice I'm not cluttering every paragraph with little brackets and page numbers. That style works for journal articles, but it kills the flow of a conversation, and this Guide is meant to read like we're talking at the kitchen table, not sitting an exam.

Here's the deal I'm making with you. Where I quote someone directly or lean heavily on a specific idea, I name them and where I'm using general concepts that are now well-established, I translate those ideas into plain language. If you want the deeper dive I've included a *'Quick Recap'* and *'Reference'* list in the back of the Guide. Think of them as signposts, not shackles. They're there so you can check the scaffolding if you're curious, not to make you wade through a swamp of citations.

This Guide is not a substitute for therapy, medication, or clinical care. If you're dealing with trauma, illness, persistent depression, anxiety that keeps hijacking your days, or anything that feels bigger than a *tough patch*, then the most courageous move is to bring in qualified help and use this Guide as a sidekick, not a primary weapon.

My job here is to keep the science honest, the language human, and the tools practical enough that you can actually use them any day. If it sounds like common sense with good manners, that's because the best science usually ends up agreeing with what our gut suspected all along.

Foreword

WHAT LIES WITHIN THESE PAGES IS MORE THAN a collection of thoughts, it's a tapestry woven from a life lived fully, threaded with triumphs, failures, happiness, loss, courage, and doubt. My journey has not been linear, the detours, the shadows, the moments I thought I would not rise from, have shaped me as much as the victories. I don't carry regret, what has been, has been. Every decision, right or wrong, was mine, every experience has led me here, to this moment of reflection, acceptance, and quiet gratitude, for all we truly have is this moment, this breath, this page, this choice.

The past has passed, the future is yet to arrive, *'now'* is where change is possible. Psychiatrist M. Scott Peck stated, *"Remember that to the uninitiated eye it would seem impossible for a stone ever to become a gem."* I have learnt that faith in the Universe is not about certainty, it's about trust. Trust that is meant for you will find you, and that which falls away was never truly yours. I no longer see the Universe as some nebulous force, I feel its presence in the quiet spaces, the synchronicities, the stillness between breaths. What we offer to the Universe, be it hope, bitterness, love, or fear, returns to us in form and feeling. That's not mysticism, it's resonance. I have lived long enough to see how the energy I put out echoes back, shaping the tone and rhythm of my life.

My reflections are fragments collected consciously or otherwise across decades, they are drawn from my time in service, in sorrow, in silence, in survival and, in surrender. Some are hard-won lessons, others are truths I resisted for far too long. All are honest.

This is a journey of discovery, of returning to myself, of recovering a quiet but unwavering faith, not in certainty, but in possibility. Within the rhythm of the Universe, the truth is that we are never as lost as we think, and always more connected than we feel. I am eternally grateful to the Universe for the chance to have lived enough life to put my learnings into words.

Thank you for joining me.

1

Daring Beyond The Shadows

You are worthy of happiness, of peace, of connection, of dreams that feel out of reach.

THERE'S A QUIET TRUTH LIVED BY MANY who have walked through darkness and decided, again and again, to keep going. If that's you, hear this clearly and with respect, you are not alone in your shadows, and you are braver than you realise for courage isn't the absence of fear, it's moving while fear watches. Courage doesn't always roar, often it looks like getting out of bed, sending one honest message, keeping an appointment, or staying in the room with your feelings long enough to hear what they are trying to say.

I've watched what happens when good people are forced to navigate hard seasons. As a friend, a partner, a colleague, and a guide, I've seen how quietly courageous survival can be. Courage isn't only about staying alive, it's about refusing to hand your story over to the worst day you've had, and daring to believe that light still counts even when you are surrounded by shadow.

Let's speak plainly. Life brings shadows. Grief rearranges the furniture. Trauma leaves you wary of your own heartbeat. Loss echoes in strange places. Depression shrinks the world. Shame tells you to disappear and, fear, betrayal, regret, compound them all. These aren't dramatic words for dramatic people, they're real experiences that arrive without asking permission. When they do, courage can feel passive, like a holding pattern you endure while waiting for the weather to clear. But real survival is active. It's resistance. It's the daily decision to show up when everything in you wants to shut down, to keep moving when the path is unclear, and to reach for help when your instinct is to hide.

This kind of courage doesn't ask for perfection or tidy answers. It asks for daring. Not grand heroics, but small, practical hope. Hope isn't pretending things will be fine by Friday. It's the decision to believe that something better is possible even before you can see how. It's trusting that this pain is not the final chapter, and acting as if there's still a page to turn. When you do that, courage becomes something sacred, you become a steward of your own strength, not because you were never broken, but because you refused to let the breaking define you.

Many of us stay in survival mode long after the danger has passed. We build walls and call them homes, we make our lives smaller and wonder why we feel cramped, we keep our hearts locked because vulnerability once invited harm. There is a season when that caution is wise. Then there comes a moment when endurance needs to become engagement, when floating is no longer enough and you decide to swim. That turning point often starts with a simple realisation, you are worthy of more than just getting through, you are worthy of peace, connection, meaning, and dreams that still feel cheeky to say out loud. Those things are not reserved for people who had an easier run, they are meant for you as well.

If you're not sure where to start, begin with your body. Survival lives in the nervous system, so give your brain evidence that you are safe enough now to live. Open a window, drink water, step into sunlight for five minutes, move until your breath deepens. This isn't wellness theatre, it's a direct signal to your biology that danger is not in the room.

And a word about courage. We romanticise it as a cinematic moment though the reality is clearer, most days it's smaller and more stubborn. It is saying *no* without a speech and *yes* without a performance. It is walking past the old trigger and choosing a different door. It rarely feels heroic, and more often than not it feels like a steady slow breath and one clean step.

Courage also learns in company. I know that asking for help can feel like standing naked in a storm. Do it anyway. Choose one person who has earned your trust and tell the plain truth about where you are. You need to be heard, and you need to hear your own voice say the words. Connection won't erase the shadows, but it will stop them from filling the entire room. If you don't have that person yet, speak to your GP, a Counsellor, or a peer group, your tribe, that understands the terrain. Being human is a team sport, whether we like it or not.

Give yourself permission to be 'in progress' as healing rarely moves in straight lines. You'll have clear days and then get blindsided by a song in a supermarket aisle. That doesn't mean you're back at the start, it means your system is clearing old echoes, and you're strong enough now to feel them without drowning. When setbacks arrive, return to basics, name what's happening, choose one controllable action, rest when you need to, restart when you can. This is how steadiness is built, through honest repetition, not grand gestures.

You'll be tempted to compare your journey to someone else's highlight reel. Don't. Some people sprint and collapse, others walk steadily and arrive upright. You have your own pace and your own path, trust it. When envy bites, turn it into information, ask what you're actually longing for in the other story. Is it connection, creativity, freedom, time, purpose? Translate that into one small move in your own life and take it.

There is also work here around forgiveness. Not as a performance, and not as a shortcut, but as a long practice of releasing what's choking your present. Sometimes that means forgiving someone with whom you can't or won't make amends. Sometimes it means forgiving yourself for choices made while you were just trying to survive. Forgiveness doesn't say it didn't matter, it says it mattered so much that you refuse to let it own your future. Set the boundaries you need, keep yourself safe, and when you're ready, loosen your grip on the story that casts you only as wounded, because you are far more than that.

Remember this, courage doesn't always feel like courage, often it feels like doubt with momentum. It feels like shaky hands making the call, it feels like hope that is almost shy. Let it be small if that's what it needs to be today, small counts, small repeats, small builds. That's how the shadows lose their authority, not because they vanish, but because you keep choosing light while they're still in view.

You didn't choose every chapter of your story, but you do get to choose how you carry them. You are allowed to want more than endurance. You are allowed to heal, you are allowed to be happy, and, you are allowed to take your time getting there. One step, one decent choice, one honest conversation at a time. Keep going. You're doing better than you think.

Courage beyond the shadows isn't a medal you wear, it's a way of moving through the world that says, '*I will keep showing up. I will keep learning. I will keep building a life I can stand in.*'

2

Fix Your Sleep, Fix Your Life

We are meant to sleep at night and be awake when the sun rises, this is how human beings evolved.

I F YOUR SLEEP IS BROKEN, EVERYTHING ELSE IS FIGHTING uphill with a flat tyre, therefore the very first step in this journey, that is, if you want a life that holds together, make sleep your first habit. Everything else orbits it whether you like that fact or not. For when you don't sleep (and I mean deep, restorative sleep), the wheels start to wobble. Quietly at first, you feel flat, foggy, and your patience thins. Motivation slips its already-weakened grip and while small problems feel personal, big ones feel unmanageable. Relationships cop the splash damage because tired people hear criticism where there was only information and react where a pause would have done the job.

That's usually when the shortcuts start whispering, a drink to smooth the edge, a pill to knock you out, another scroll because lying there feels unbearable. The lift is short and the slide is long, mood swings widen, behaviour gets scratchy, shame joins the conversation and the next night is worse. That's the loop. Break it and half your life starts behaving again.

Sleep isn't just rest, it's a nightly housekeeping shift your brain refuses to outsource. While you sleep, the system files the day's memories, clears metabolic rubbish, settles emotional charge, and rehearses tomorrow's decisions. It's why *sleep on it* has survived every era and every culture. A good night pulls you back toward centre and makes the next choice cleaner, kinder, and less dramatic.

Sleep isn't one thing you drop into and climb out of, it's a rhythm your brain runs all night long, a kind of quiet shift work where different crews come on at different times to keep you functional, sane, and recognisably yourself.

Non-REM sleep takes the first watch and does the unglamorous heavy lifting, slowing brain activity, dropping heart rate and blood pressure, repairing tissue, calming inflammation, clearing metabolic rubbish from the brain, and stabilising emotional tone so you don't wake up already carrying yesterday like a hangover. This is where deep slow-wave sleep lives, the stage that restores physical energy, consolidates straightforward memory, steadies mood, and resets your stress system so small problems don't feel like personal threats.

As the night rolls on, *REM (Rapid Eye Movement) sleep* gradually takes over, the brain lights up again while the body stays safely offline, and this is where emotional processing, creativity, insight, and meaning-making happen, memories are woven together rather than just stored, sharp emotional edges are softened, and experiences are integrated into a story you can live with instead of react to.

Movement, mindfulness, and healthy (non-processed)food quietly support this system. Daytime exercise improves blood flow and gives your brain the oxygen and glucose it loves. Simple mindfulness or breath work turns down the mental committee that tries to convene at 2a.m. Food that supports serotonin (feel good hormone) production lays the groundwork for melatonin (sleep chemical) later on. Think real meals with protein and sensible carbohydrates, eggs, dairy, legumes, lean meats. No magic powders required, just chemistry behaving as designed.

Routine matters as much as duration, for humans evolved to sleep when it's dark and wake when light returns. Nothing fundamental has changed. Aim for a consistent sleep window, even on weekends, as earlier nights and earlier rises will beat a late binge of screens followed by a groggy start every time. Caffeine is useful until lunchtime, after that many of us pay for it at eleven. Alcohol sedates but fragments sleep. Nicotine stimulates. Doomscrolling lights up threat circuits that have no business running at bedtime.

About an hour before sleep, hand the controls to your inner manager, providing short, civil instructions you can obey while tired. Lights down, screens out of the bedroom, warm shower, notebook open. Write one line about what mattered today and one line about tomorrow's first task. That tiny ritual tells your brain the day is parked. Soft music is fine, warm drink is fine, however remember you're building a reliable landing strip, not a spa retreat. Make the room a cave. Cool, dark, and quiet blocks light leaks. Put the phone outside the door and use a cheap alarm clock. If you share a bed with a restless sleeper, separate top sheets and a heavier doona can save the peace. If a pet treats 3 a.m. like a roller park, give them their own bed in a separate room with the door closed, that's love with boundaries.

When sleep won't come, stop wrestling the mattress, and if you're awake and wired after about twenty minutes, get up, keep the lights low, read something (non-electronic), something gentle. Stretch, sit and breathe and when your eyelids start to sag, return to bed. You're teaching your brain that bed equals sleep and comfort, not rumination and combat. A slow body scan helps, starting at the toes and softening each muscle group on the out-breath, and if numbers help, try four in, seven hold, eight out. No mysticism here, just signalling safety.

Shift workers, carers, and new parents run on a different clock. You are not failing, you're tired. Anchor sleep to a routine rather than a time. Darken the room as if it were night, wear sunglasses on the way home from night shift so daylight doesn't shout at your body clock. Nap with intent, short and early in your wake window and protect two things without apology; a wind-down ritual and an honest block of sleep whenever the chance appears.

Mindfulness earns its keep at night because worry collapses time, it drags yesterday's mess and tomorrow's unknowns into the same pile. Five minutes of sitting with yourself can stop that merger. Eyes closed, feel the breath, label thoughts as thinking and let them pass, remember you're not chasing enlightenment, you're practicing the skill of not now, we are aiming for *now we rest*.

Nutrition helps without becoming precious. Dinner doesn't need to be clever, eat real (non-processed) food, keep it earlier if reflux is an issue, have your last meal, snack or munchies no less than four hours before you go to bed. If hunger wakes you at 3am, it's called water, but only a bit, you don't want the next wake cycle to be emptying your bladder, so hydrate through the day so you're not up all night visiting the bathroom. Save the heroic workouts for earlier hours, as hard training late can keep some people wired. If you must train late, cool down longer and land gently.

Protect the morning light master switch. Get outside within an hour of waking, even for five minutes, as sunlight through the eyes sets your clock, lifts mood. Move your body a little, walk, stretch, save the heavy stuff for later.

Catastrophising turns one rough night into a long term prophecy as *Rumination* swaps your thoughts around and around. Learn some mindfulness techniques to calm your mind, as that shift lowers arousal and makes sleep more likely. If poor sleep drags on for weeks, if snoring or choking wakes you, or if mood drops hard, speak to your GP. Getting help isn't weakness. It's maintenance for the machine you live in.

Tie sleep into the rest of your practices. Gratitude grows when you thank last night you for turning the lights out on time. Savouring grows when you notice how morning light feels on your face. Journalling grows when you close the day with two plain lines and let the Guide hold them. Forgiveness grows when you stop punishing yourself for not being a robot and choose rest over self-attack.

If you want a plan for tonight, keep it boring. Cut caffeine after midday, eat a sane dinner four hours before you lay your head on your pillow, dim the lights an hour before bed, phone out of the room. Have a warm shower, read a page or even one line of this Guide. Take two minutes to slow your breathing with lights out at the time you chose earlier in the day. If you wake, be kind and repeat. Tomorrow morning, step into the light and move. Then do it again.

Sleep is not a lazy gap, it's a highly active set of brain states that repairs tissue, calibrates emotion, and cements learning. Put it first and everything else becomes easier to do well. You get nicer, you think cleaner, you become a better partner, parent, mate, colleague and a better friend to yourself. What I am offering you is not hype or eastern mysticism, it's how humans work. Treat sleep as non-negotiable and the rest of your *Growth* has solid ground to stand on.

3

Start Where the Light Is Already On

You do not need to become a different person.

START WHERE THE LIGHT IS ALREADY ON, by concentrating on your strengths, the things you genuinely do well, even if you can only name one today, it isn't vanity, it's fuel. When you place attention on a real ability and put it to work, your energy lifts, your posture changes, and something subtle but important shifts in how you move through the day. You don't need a crowd or a medal. You need one honest strength and the decision to use it on purpose.

Most of us were raised on a curriculum of deficiency. I was raised to hunt flaws and treat competence as background noise, to stay within my station of life and don't stick you head above the crowd and that, for a long time, left me lopsided. You become a skilled critic of yourself and a poor witness to your own capability. The antidote isn't pretending you're exceptional at everything. It's disciplined noticing, learning to see what already works, then giving it a job.

A strength isn't a party trick, it's a reliable pattern of thought or behaviour that creates value under pressure. If you steady a room when tempers rise, that's a strength. If you can untangle a problem without escalating it, that's a strength. If people feel calmer around you within a minute, that's a strength. None of these need applause, they're quiet machines, and when you switch them on deliberately, outcomes change.

Begin with evidence, don't collect flattering adjectives, collect proof. Think of three moments in the past three months where things could have gone sideways and didn't, rebuild them like a detective. What exactly did you do? What did you refuse to do? Which question, decision, or tone shifted the result? The mechanics of those outcomes is important as your nervous system trusts data far more than praise.

Once you've named the strength, aim it. Targeted strengths move boulders. Untargeted strengths become decorations. Pick one live problem at home or work and ask, how does my strength touch this? The goal isn't to feel impressive, it's to change the state of play.

Expect resistance. The road most travelled systems like you best in the role they're used to, even when that role costs you. Some people are oddly invested in chaos because it makes them feel needed. Hold your line. You're not responsible for preserving dysfunction so others stay comfortable.

Feedback helps if you choose the right sources. Ask three people who want the best for you, not the most from you. Keep the question simple. *Where do you see me at my best?* Don't argue with the answers. You're collecting vantage points, not cross-examining witnesses. When two or more people agree, treat it as a map reference and test it in real conditions.

Every strength has a shadow, as warmth can slide into people-pleasing, courage can tip into bulldozing, precision can drift into perfectionism and anxiety. The fix isn't to abandon the strength, it's to frame it with purpose and boundary. Ask yourself one steadying question. *When does this serve the mission, and when does it serve my ego?* That question will save you time, money, and a few apologies you'd rather avoid.

Watch the comparison trap, as someone else's highlight reel can make your solid competence look dull, ignore it, as most lives improve through ordinary strengths used consistently. Reliability builds families, teams, and neighbourhoods that breathe, it also builds the only confidence that survives scrutiny, the earned kind.

If you're rebuilding after a rough season, start smaller again, find one strength that survived. Maybe you still listen well, maybe you show up on time, maybe you can make a good cup of tea and sit without fixing. Don't sneer at small hinges, they swing big doors. You're not trying to become who you were, you're learning how to carry what you know with less waste.

Teach your strengths to work together, pair analysis with empathy, pair steadiness with decisive action at the right moment. Think of them as hands passing the work. If your dominant hand is vision, your supporting hand needs follow-through if your dominant hand is calm, your support is timely clarity.

Bring your body and attention into the process for when you use a strength deliberately, notice what happens in your system. Does your chest loosen? Does your thinking widen? That feedback tells you you're on track. When you avoid using a strength you know you have, notice the cost. You'll feel a drag, a small resentment toward yourself, a sense you're living under your size.

Give your strength a weekly job. Write it at the top of a page on Sunday night, keep a simple record, one line each evening about where you used it and what happened. No literature required. *This week I'll use calm to de-escalate three tense moments. This week I'll use clarity to ask early questions that prevent rework.* Keep it countable and within reach. Repetition lays wiring you can trust when the week gets noisy. Over a month those lines become a map. You'll see where the strength pays, where it needs a boundary, and where another strength needs to step in.

As your strengths get cleaner, let them upgrade your environment. Decline roles that only value your rescue reflex. Say yes to work that uses your best patterns early, not as a last resort. Build relationships that recognise and reciprocate.

You don't need to become a different person to achieve *Growth*. You need to become a truer version of the person you already are, less scattered and more directed. Name the strength, aim it at something real, measure the change, learn from the shadow. Then do it again tomorrow.

Use one chosen strength at a time. It won't look dramatic, but it is how you move toward coherence, being grounded and remaining strong.

4

Survival Beyond The Shadows

Survival Taught You More Than Comfort Ever Did.

SURVIVING BEYOND THE SHADOWS DOESN'T MEAN FEAR packs up and moves interstate and it doesn't mean the past turns into a tidy museum with polite plaques and exit signs. It means you learn to walk with what happened without letting it steer. You notice the shadow, you acknowledge its presence and, in small stubborn ways, you refuse to let it write your ending. That isn't denial, its authorship, building boundaries in a life that honours what you've been through without becoming imprisoned by it, for the hard seasons didn't break you, they trained you.

So, what does *Surviving Beyond The Shadows* look like in the real world? It looks like boundaries, the ones that protect your energy and emotional space, not the barbed-wire type flung up when you're exhausted, but clean, repeatable ones you can hold. *'I can talk at seven, not now. I can help on Saturday. I can't fix that issue. I won't be spoken to like that.'* They aren't punishments, they're conditions for connection, they keep you human enough to stay in the room without disappearing or exploding. They look like speaking truths you once swallowed. You don't need a megaphone, you need one sentence. *'That hurt. I'm not available for that anymore. Here's what I need going forward.'* The first time you put one in place it feels like walking a cracked plank over open water. The second time your voice steadies and by the tenth time you realise truth was never the enemy, you were simply out of practice.

Surviving Beyond The Shadows also looks like asking for help, not as a confession of weakness but as an act of strength. Find one decent human who speaks plainly, an old friend, a steady family member, a Counsellor who talks like a person not a pamphlet. You don't earn medals for dragging boulders alone.

Connection isn't a luxury, it's protective gear for healing, and healing moves faster in company.

It also looks like Rest and Grace, even when the critic in your head says you haven't earned them. You don't have to be wrecked to deserve a breather as rest isn't a reward, it's maintenance and grace isn't indulgence, it's fuel. Use the same tone you'd use with a mate who's had enough. Brief. Factual. Decent. *'That's enough for today. Eat. Sleep. Try again tomorrow.'*

Surviving Beyond The Shadows means pursuing what lights you up while the old voices mutter about how you shouldn't, let them mutter, you're busy living. Start small if that's all you've got. Ten minutes with the guitar, a walk near water or trees. Your happiness doesn't need a business plan, it needs oxygen.

It also means reclaiming happiness in moments the past tries to stain. The shadow will have opinions about your laughter, as if joy makes you disloyal to your history. Ignore it. You're allowed to smile in the kitchen without consulting a committee of ghosts. Pain isn't a vow, it's a chapter, as happiness doesn't erase what happened, it interrupts the shadow's grip on today.

Survival isn't one grand gesture, it's thousands of small ones that add up to a quiet revolution. Every time you choose a boundary over resentment, honesty over performance, rest over punishment, you're not just surviving, you're building *Growth* in your life with your fingerprints all over it.

If you're reading this, thinking, *'that sounds like someone stronger than me,'* let me push back. You've already survived more than your mind gives you credit for and the evidence is simple and unavoidable. *You're here, in this moment right now.*

Strength doesn't always feel like fireworks, often it looks like getting out of bed when the forecast in your chest says stay under. It looks like sending one message instead of disappearing, it looks like choosing water when the old routine offers something rougher. Give yourself the credit you'd give a stranger for the same effort.

Let's be honest about the terrain. The shadows don't evaporate because you declared a new era, they test your fences. They show up when you're tired and whisper that nothing ever changes, they drag you back toward rehearsals, the argument you never won, the apology you never got, the decision you wish you could unmake. You don't need amnesia. You need jurisdiction, *'Not in this room. Not right now.'* Put the scene back where it belongs, in your history, not in your hands, repair it with your actual voice to an actual human. Otherwise, stop holding court in your skull, a Courtroom in the head never adjourns.

There's a practical piece here about self-talk. *Fire the inner prosecutor. Hire a manager.* The prosecutor rants in absolutes. *'Always. Never. Failure.'* The manager issues verbs. *'Walk for ten minutes. Eat real food first. Wait twenty minutes before replying.'* Managers don't insult, they get you across the line.

The shadow will tell you you're too broken, too late, too tired, too complicated. Smile at it, not with mockery, but with recognition. *'Of course you'd say that.'* Shadows stretch ordinary problems until they look like national emergencies. Your job isn't to out-argue them, it's to keep moving in the light you've got, feet on the floor, shoulders down, chin level. You're not auditioning for the role of *healed person*, you're practicing being a *decent, steady one*, that's enough.

There will be days you backslide. You'll take the call you shouldn't, you'll write the message you regret, you'll replay the scene until your jaw aches. That's OK, it's alright, for you can lock away your sticky note reminder to *notice sooner, repair sooner, reset sooner. 'That was the old move. Here's the new one.'* The win in *Growth* isn't about perfection, nor the speed of recovery, it's getting there under your own terms.

If you need an anchor for messy moments, use this rhythm. *See what's actually here. Name what your body is doing. Choose the smallest clean act. Move your hands on something real for two minutes.* It isn't glamorous. It works.

Keep your humour, the jaw-loosening kind that lets air back into the room. *'Alright ego, off the tools.'* A half-smile can break a spiral. And if laughter's too far away, aim for a slow exhale that sounds like the start of one.

Here's the truth I want you carrying. The shadows don't get to keep you, they can ride along if they must, buckled in the back seat, windows up, no DJ privileges. They don't get the wheel, that belongs to the part of you that keeps showing up. Tired maybe, wary perhaps, but still here, for you are daring, you are still reaching, even when the light feels like a rumour. You don't have to believe every day, you just have to keep walking forward, one step, then another. That's the method of continued survival on repeat. And if you wobble, if you sit on the curb and curse the sky, that's fine, time will wait with you. Then you'll stand, square your shoulders and take the next small true step and call it what it is, *Victory*, and keep walking, as you're not done, for *You Are Not Alone*.

5

Finding The Wisdom To Try Again

You may not know exactly what lies ahead, but your resilience is your guiding star.

SOMETIMES LIFE FEELS LIKE A SERIES OF SHADOWS, long stretches of darkness broken by brief, stubborn light, and if you're in the shadows again you already know the scrape of crawling your way out because you've done it before.

This chapter is for the mornings you stare at the ceiling wondering how to be a person again, for the afternoons you sit in the car a few minutes longer because the next move feels heavy, and for the nights your eyes are back to the ceiling, promising yourself you'll try again tomorrow.

There's usually a tug in the chest when you become aware that it's time to emerge from whatever shadow is holding you, sometimes it's barely a whisper, sometimes it arrives wearing muddy boots, and sometimes it turns up as a mate's text at exactly the right moment. It feels familiar because you've answered it before, and it feels frightening because you remember the effort it took. Don't sprint past that signal. Acknowledge it. There's dignity in saying, *'I hear you.'*

You might not be ready for a hero's journey, but you can put both feet on the floor. Call it hope if you want, call it a nudge from the Universe if that suits you better, but either way, treat it as real. Trying again is less romance and more choreography, as the mind wants a grand plan, but the body wants one clean move. Choose something small and deliberate and do it like you mean it. A short walk in real air. Two sentences that you've been avoiding. Ten minutes with the guitar, a chapter of this Guide, or listening to your favourite playlist. Frame it as a step, not a leap. Steps give you proof, and proof is the antidote to despair. You're not telling yourself you can do it, you're showing yourself that you already did.

If you can, start with your body, let the shoulders drop, soften the jaw, lengthen the exhale, look far enough that your visual field widens and the shadow shrinks by a metre. *Drink a glass of water. Eat something with protein.* These can sound like insults to a complicated life, but they're scaffolding, and scaffolding holds you steady while you reach for the next rung. Brains believe bodies more than speeches, so give your nervous system evidence that there's room to move.

Before you push forward, turn around for a moment and look back without a whip in your hand. Be mindful that every climb leaves marks, some are scars that itch when the weather changes, others are muscles you didn't have last time. Ask yourself three plain questions, *'What did I learn? How did I grow? What strength showed up when I needed it?'* Write the answers on a scrap of paper or say them into the quiet. That isn't self-help theatre, it's how you turn burdens into beacons so they can light the next stretch of track. You don't earn extra points for doing this alone. Courage isn't isolation in a cape, it's an ordinary human reaching for a steady hand. Tell someone you trust that you're stepping toward the light again. You don't need a speech, just something simple like, *'I'm coming up for air and I could use company.'* Let them bring what they can, a listening ear, a lift, a healthy meal, or quiet company on a couch. Connection isn't weakness, it's wisdom about how mammals heal.

Expect the light to feel different this time, it might be softer, or a little further away, but steadier once you find it. Every return carries new information, you know where the floor dips, you recognise the voice in your head that sounds like you but is really fear doing a bad impression, and you've learnt which rooms give you oxygen and which ones take it away. Use that knowledge, adjust the route, as you're not the person who fell last time, you're the person who learnt on the way down and on the way back up.

Keep your self-talk honest and useful. *Walk to the letterbox and back. Wait twenty minutes before replying to the email.* There will be days when the shadow wins a round, you'll stay in bed too long, scroll yourself into a fog, or say the sharp thing and wish you hadn't. Alright. *Notice sooner. Repair sooner. Reset sooner.*

Keep a short evening ritual that proves you're moving. Three lines in a notebook will do. *What mattered today? Why did it matter?* It might be tiny. *'I walked to the corner. I answered one email. I laughed at the dog being ridiculous. I felt morning light on my face. I cleared the table of clutter. I listened to music that calmed my soul.'*

The point is, when your mind tries to sell you the story that nothing ever changes, you'll have receipts. Though these don't solve your life, they give your life somewhere to stand while you solve the next part. Try to keep one space where you can breathe without asking permission from a screen.

Let others help you calibrate. Ask a Counsellor, a mentor, or a mate to check your blind spots, not to run your life but to help you hear your own voice under the noise. When care is offered, let it land. You're not a burden for needing company, you're someone who understands that wisdom grows faster in shared air.

Be ready for the brain's old tricks, it will tell you that you're late, broken, behind, too much, or not enough. Smile at it the way you would at that dog being ridiculous. Loud isn't the same as true. If you need a counter-spell, try this quietly and often, *'I'm not behind, I'm arriving. I'm not broken, I'm healing. I'm not too much. I'm alive.'* Corny works when it's gentle and repeated. Your cells get the hint.

Trying again isn't just survival, it's wisdom it's defiance building resilience. It's refusing to be defined by the lowest point on your graph. It's a quiet declaration that your spirit hasn't gone out. You might not know what the next kilometre holds, but you know enough to take the next step, and that's all any of us ever get.

So, step toward the light, one deliberate courageous footfall at a time. Let each emergence rewrite your story by inches. You are not the darkness of the shadow you passed through, you are the person who keeps returning, a little wiser, steadier and kinder each round. Keep going. The sky is still there. You may not know exactly what lies ahead, but your resilience is already doing the guiding, because history only repeats when you refuse to learn from it.

6

Self-Talk That Doesn't Sabotage You

Talk to yourself like someone you're responsible for.

T HE TONE OF YOUR INNER VOICE DECIDES how hard life feels. If the voice in your head were a person, would you put them on your team? Or would you tell them to take a long walk and stop shouting across the lounge like a shock jock running on instant coffee?

Most of us carry an inner commentator who talks big, knows little, and turns every speed bump into a manifesto, then has the hide to call it motivation while you sit there calming the alarms it set off before you can do anything useful. The plain truth is that the tone you use on yourself shifts your biochemistry, and your biochemistry shapes your behaviour. Which is why snarling at yourself isn't *'tough love'*, it's a threat signal your brain takes seriously, raising heart rate, tightening breath, narrowing attention, and powering down the clever part of you while the primitive gear grabs the wheel. Whereas, speaking to yourself like a decent manager, brief, factual, steady, brings the system back to a state where you can think better and act cleaner, not because you suddenly believe in yourself, but because you have stopped dodging imaginary punches long enough to get on with the day.

Positive thinking on its own is cheap fuel, because it burns fast and leaves you stranded the moment life pushes back, while positive self-worth grows much more reliably when you can see yourself doing what you said you would do, even in small ways, and especially in small ways. I'm not proposing glitter pen affirmations or motivational posters that make you want to throw your kettle, because what we are building here is an internal voice that gets you across the line without breaking plates, and the goal isn't hype, it is honesty with manners, which means the first move is a demotion. Fire your inner prosecutor, the one who loves absolute language like never, useless, failure, and keeps a perfect scrapbook of your worst three minutes, because that voice is not truth, it is a style of thinking, and its favourite trick is to sell you the lie that volume beats accuracy while it plugs your inner microphone straight into your threat response. Self-respect isn't a trophy you win at the end of the process, it is the tone you use at the beginning, and underneath that sits biology you can work with, because language is a lever on the *Limbic System*, the emotional machinery that links what you feel to what your body does, which is why a harsh sentence can spike stress in your chest and a steady sentence can give your nervous system room to breathe and your decisions room to improve.

One of the most underrated tools in this whole game is naming what is happening without becoming it, because when you place a label on the state, fast heart, tight jaw, story of rejection, urge to bite, you cool the circuit and hand the wheel back to your *Prefrontal Cortex*, the executive decision making part that actually knows how to drive, and that is why the first sentence matters so much. *'I'm useless'*, locks you in a box and then asks you to perform in it, while *'I'm flooded and I need a break'*, opens a window you can climb through, and the difference is not softness, it is usefulness.

Where your attention goes, your day goes, and your questions are software updates, so be careful what prompts you keep feeding yourself. Ask your mind, *'Why am I like this?'* and it will gladly produce a highlight reel that proves the prosecution's case, because it loves being right more than it loves you being well, but ask instead, *'What would help by ten per cent?'* and you give your system a job it can actually complete. You will need different settings across the day because humans are not consistent machines and anyone who tells you otherwise is selling something. Mornings are a factory reset for many of us, a little fog, a little dread, and the urge to doomscroll dressed up as keeping up, so don't negotiate with the gremlin before coffee. Phone down, kettle on, shoes on, and whatever tiny script you can repeat without thinking will beat a dozen philosophies you cannot remember when your brain is still booting. Mid arvo, the sugar and screens gremlin arrives in a clown suit and tells you a biscuit will fix your existential questions, so make a deal that isn't stupid, tea first, five minutes outside, and if you still want the biscuit after the walk, have it like an adult and don't turn it into a referendum on your character. Evenings can turn into a courtroom if you let them, with your inner commentator listing everything you didn't do, weren't, or should've foreseen twelve years ago, so shut the court down before it opens, write two lines in a notebook, what mattered today and why, not a diary for the ages, just proof for your nervous system that the day held good weight as well as difficulty, because there is a time to review failure and there is also a time to sit in the same room as your wins, without trying to evict them.

Yes, you will slip, you will let the wrong voice run the room, and you will find yourself practicing eloquent self-contempt in the shower like you're auditioning for a tragedy that never got funded. However, when you catch it, don't launch a second script about how you should be past this by now, because that is just the prosecutor wearing a fake moustache. Change the sentence, not your citizenship. *'I'm being theatrical, back to useful,'* is a good reset, and a little wit helps disarm the drama. *'Alright mate, enough poetry,'* can be all it takes to break the spell and return you to action.

Small language tweaks move the needle more than grand speeches, and the simplest one is swapping *'I am'* for *'I'm noticing because I'm anxious'* turns anxiety into your identity, while *'I'm noticing anxiety'* reminds your mind that a state is moving through you rather than defining you, which makes it easier to tolerate and easier to steer.

Watch your self-talk when you succeed as well, because the same inner critic who punishes you for not suceeding will try to punish you for winning, *'lucky, wasn't that hard, wait till they see the real you,'* and you don't have to argue with that voice, you can thank it for its outdated service and keep the win anyway. *'I did that, not perfect, but good enough to count,'* is humility done properly, because humility isn't pretending it didn't happen, it is taking the right sized nod and getting back to work without turning your life into an awards night.

Keep some privacy around your self-talk because not every doubt deserves public oxygen, and if you outsource your confidence to a crowd your inner voice will bend with the weather, which is a miserable way to live. Build a small, sober internal voice you trust more than *likes*, let a handful of steady people check your blind spots when you need it, and don't turn the internet into your panel of judges, because crowds are noisy and the nervous system hates noise.

If harsh self-talk has lived in your head for years, expect a protest when you change the tone, because the old voice will accuse you of going soft and losing your edge, and this is where you smile. Edges are easy, steadiness is rare. You do not improve by terrorising yourself. You improve by telling the truth in a way you can act on tomorrow as well as today, and if you wouldn't let a stranger speak to your kid like that, don't let your inner voice speak to you like that either, because cruelty is not discipline, it is just cruelty with a new label.

When you feel your self-talk getting spiky, change the physical state first, because words chosen in a calmer body land better and last longer. Stand up, change rooms, step outside, let light hit your face, move until your breath reminds you, you're human, not an avatar, then let the voice speak again, because the brain believes the body more than it believes speeches, and a regulated body makes it far easier to choose a regulated sentence.

You are not trying to become the world's most positive person. You are trying to become someone whose inner voice makes courage cheaper, humility easier, and emotional repairs faster, which is the whole point of *Growth* that actually sticks.

Talk to yourself like someone you're responsible for, not like a client you're trying to impress, not like a rival you're trying to beat, and not like a criminal you're trying to break. Because responsible people don't coddle and they don't crush, they give clear instructions, keep small promises, apologise quickly when they miss, and return to useful without theatre. Do that often enough and your inner room becomes a place you can work in, not perfect, liveable, and that is where a better life with *Growth* gets built.

7

Excuses Are Comfortable — Progress Isn't

Momentum isn't a mood, it's what happens when you return.

THE STORIES THAT PROTECT YOU TODAY are often the ones quietly costing you tomorrow. Life moves fast, sometimes faster than your nervous system would prefer, and while you don't control interest rates, traffic, or whether someone else turns up carrying their bad morning into your day, you do control more than you often give yourself credit for. Including, what time your phone goes to sleep, whether you move your body before the world gets loud, the tone you bring into a tense room, and whether you choose to speak steadily when things feel messy. Somewhere around two in the morning, when the house is quiet and there's no audience to perform for, you already know this, that something needs to shift, not the habits you inherited, not the stories that raised you, not the rules that once kept the peace, but yours, and that realisation stings because it puts the steering wheel back in your hands.

Most of us have spent time in the *Temple of Excuses*, a grand old building with high ceilings where even flimsy reasons echo like wisdom where '*not today, too risky, too late, too expensive, and too complicated'* sound thoughtful rather than avoidant. No one sets out to worship delay, it just happens slowly, a candle lit here, another there, until you find yourself trusting that the Universe is taking notes and will let you know when conditions are perfect. Along the way you collect explanations the way a junk drawer collects batteries, a few for health, a matched set for difficult conversations, and a deluxe edition for money and work, and after a while they stop feeling like choices and start feeling like air. The Temple once kept you safe, it helped you get through rough seasons, but it charges a tax, paid in stalled momentum, heavier moods, and a nervous system that's forgotten how to try without bracing for impact.

The Temple didn't go up overnight, it started with small outs learned early, ways to dodge discomfort or buy time, and over the years it expanded to fit every chapter of your life, because your brain is efficient and risk-averse and would rather conserve energy than gamble on uncertainty. Stick with it long enough and you grow armour to match, a protective shell that keeps criticism out, which feels like relief, but it keeps help out too, which is costly. People who care struggle to get through, new ideas bounce off, and you end up defended and stuck, safe but static, like a turtle wearing a helmet it no longer needs.

The Temple also has a choir, familiar voices who share your frame of reference because agreement feels like safety, and while they're not bad people, they act as mirrors, and if every mirror reflects the same image, change starts to feel like betrayal. That's why widening the circle matters, not dramatically, just enough to include one person who wants the best for you rather than the most comfort, someone you can tell about one small shift you're making and who'll check in like a human, not a supervisor.

Here's the quieter truth, you don't need to tear the Temple down, you can simply walk across the street. There's a smaller place there, no marble, no incense, just a chalkboard menu and a bell over the door, the *Café of Possibilities*. It's always open and it doesn't serve sermons, only choices, and you don't need the seven-course tasting plate because one dish is plenty. Order one change and eat it slowly, let it settle, and when you're ready, come back and order another. One small change a month is enough to shift a life, not glamorous, not Instagram-friendly, but reliable, which is how real momentum is built.

Expect a wobble, because your system prefers the old script and some people liked the version of you who never made waves, and that's alright, just keep returning to the counter. Momentum isn't created by force or enthusiasm, it grows through repetition, by showing up again after a miss, again after doubt, again after the familiar pull of *'Not Today'*.

It helps to remember that some of the Temple's power is biological rather than moral, because poor sleep, constant stress, and bright screens at midnight turn even sensible brains into skilled excuse salespeople. Looking after your internal chemistry isn't self-improvement theatre, it's maintenance. Protecting sleep, getting daylight on your face in the morning, moving most days and eating food that grew somewhere and wasn't thrown together in a lab, because a rested brain is less dramatic and more useful. When you run yourself to *Frazzle*, attention thins, memory frays, patience unravels and everything feels harder than it needs to be.

You don't become a new person first, you act like the person you're becoming and let your brain update the file afterward. Keep small promises to yourself and announce them after you've done the thing, not before, because confidence grows out of evidence, not speeches. Keep humour in your kit as well, not the biting kind that leaves marks, but the jaw-loosening kind that lets a room breathe, so when your old internal monologue turns up dressed as logic, you can smile, say *'nice try mate,'* and carry on.

If you slip, skip the theatre, because the moment you start rehearsing a tragedy about failure, you'll find yourself back under stained glass, so change the next five minutes instead. That's the trick, not to attain perfection but enhance the speed of repair, returning before the gap widens.

Before you step fully into the Café, take one last look at the Temple, because it did its job once and helped you survive a rough season, and you can acknowledge that without staying. Across the street the bell is still ringing, the menu is fresh, and they only serve what you can actually swallow. Walk in, order one change, eat slowly, notice the win, and come back tomorrow, because you'll feel the shift first in your chest, then in your calendar, and then in the way people relax when you walk into a room. That's the quiet dividend of leaving the *Temple of Excuses* and becoming a regular at the *Café of Possibilities.*

8

What You're Holding Is What's Holding You

The fastest way to recreate yesterday is to keep misreading today.

YOUR PAST IS A PRISON WITH THE DOOR ALREADY OPEN. I learned early that stuff happens, sometimes unfairly, sometimes brutally, sometimes in ways that leave marks long after the moment has passed. You can keep doing laps inside your skull, polishing old injuries like family heirlooms, or you can walk out the door and feel the weather on your face.

You can't erase what happened in the past, but you can decide whether it gets to live rent-free in your head. That decision is what *Letting Go* actually is, a deliberate choice about where your attention, and therefore your life, will live. Letting go isn't weakness, it's making room for something better.

Letting go is not about forgetting, excusing, or pretending you didn't know better. It's about deciding that the past no longer gets to drive the car while you're trying to live in the present. It's about releasing the grip of anger, shame, and disappointment so they stop setting your tone, stealing your energy, and quietly shaping your choices from behind the scenes. Most of the real work of forgiveness is inward. Not because you were the villain, but because you're the one still paying the bill. When we don't forgive ourselves, we keep paying in guilt and shame, and those currencies bankrupt clear thinking fast. They narrow your options, distort your memory, and convince you that punishment equals accountability. It doesn't. Punishment produces secrecy. Repair produces wisdom. Self-forgiveness restores balance not by erasing what happened, but by helping you stand in the now with your eyes open and your feet steady, able to act instead of rehearse.

Let's be precise. Forgiveness isn't amnesia and it isn't weakness. It's the decision to stop paying interest on an old debt so you can fund your future instead. You still remember exactly what happened, but you just refuse to let it continue to lease space in your head. Keep the lesson, install the inner boundary and move on with the business of living. No incense. No halo. Just an adult decision about where your attention goes.

Reality is that most people run a permanent Courtroom in their skull, evidence exhibits, closing arguments, imaginary cross-examinations, and it sits 24/7. This is known as *Rumination*, and it can feel productive, even righteous, but it never ends well because the Judge is always you and the verdict never sticks. Swap the inner Courtroom for an inner Workshop. In a workshop you repair, replace parts, set tolerances, and throw out what's broken without ceremony. That shift, from prosecuting to fixing, is the backbone of letting go. The past becomes raw material, not a museum you're forced to tour daily.

Start with the hardest customer, yourself. *'Self-forgiveness'* isn't a slogan and it isn't a spa day. Used properly, guilt is a smoke alarm, it a keeps you morally and ethically alert, gets you out, and lets you make the house safer, it is not meant to be your landlord. We've all have/had guilt, and you'll be tempted to punish yourself in an attempt to balance the ledger. Don't. Punishment doesn't produce insight, it produces hiding in the shadows. Amends produce insight, so fix what you can, apologise where needed, repay if there's a debt, repair what's repairable. Then make future payments in changed behaviour. If trust took a hit, rebuild it with small, boring, repeatable actions, not dramatic vows. You're not chasing absolution from an invisible jury, you're becoming someone you can trust to drive your own life.

Bring the body into the work. Old anger and regret don't live only in sentences, they live in shoulders, jaw, breath, and sleep. Pair letting-go with movement so your nervous system gets the memo. Walk until your pulse lifts, take ten slow exhales with the jaw unclenched, then lift, swim, stretch, or hang from a bar and feel your grip. You're telling your body, in a language it believes, that the danger has passed and the punch you keep bracing for landed years ago. Thinking improves when the body stops guarding against ghosts.

Forgiving others sits nearby, but it's a different job. You can forgive and never reconcile, you can forgive and still go to court, you can forgive and keep your distance forever. Forgiveness is ownership of your inner world. Reconciliation is about their pattern of behaviour and the conditions of access. If someone has a long résumé of not keeping you safe, compassion doesn't require proximity. You can see through a fence, open the gate if behaviour changes, and close it again without drama when it doesn't.

Here's the rub. Anger practiced becomes a personality, and resentment rehearsed turns into identity. Hold the hot coal long enough and you forget you're the one gripping it. Meanwhile, the people or events that hurt you keep throwing pity parties in your mind, with free drinks and an open microphone. Letting go isn't a favour to them, it's an eviction notice you serve on your own behalf.

A lot of what weighs us down isn't new pain, it's old weight we keep lifting. Arguments replayed in the shower, imaginary comebacks delivered to audiences that don't exist, screenshots stored for righteous fury later. That clutter is only heavy while you're holding it. Set it down. If something needs a boundary, set it, if it needs a conversation, have it once, calmly, with your actual voice, not ten times with the prosecution living in your skull. If it's neither, bin it, and you'll feel oxygen return.

Try this. Grab an ordinary glass and fill it with water, then hold it straight out in front of you. At first it's easy. After a minute, still manageable. After five minutes your arm aches, your shoulder complains, and soon enough your hand starts to shake. The problem isn't the glass, it's how long you've been holding it. Now tip the glass upside down and empty it. Suddenly it weighs almost nothing. Keep holding the empty glass long enough and it becomes heavy again. Put it gently down and let your arm fall back to your side. That's letting go. The same thing happens in your head. The longer you hold onto something, the heavier it becomes, regardless of what it actually is.

Cultivate a non-stick mind and let thoughts land and slide off instead of letting the last one bully the next. When a barb hits, look at something real in the room for two seconds and bring your attention back the way you'd coax a puppy, not scold a criminal. And for the love of accuracy, stop letting yesterday's knowledge block today's truth. If facts change, change with them. Being wrong isn't fatal, but being welded to rightness, is.

Letting go is not permission for other people to walk through you, it pairs beautifully with boundaries. Short, behavioural, repeatable ones. *'I won't be spoken to like that. I can help Saturday, not today. This topic is for a phone call, not text.'* You're not punishing anyone, you're protecting the conditions under which you can stay decent to yourself.

If what you're carrying isn't drama but grief, call it by its proper name. Grieve on purpose with walks, a few honest pages, a Counsellor who speaks human. Grief clears the channel, grievance clogs it. Let go and you can feel the difference in your jaw. However, dropping your baggage is only half the work. The other half is cleaning the glass you look through, because the fastest way to recreate yesterday is too misread today as the mind loves *Affective Forecasting*, predicting tomorrow's feelings using today's mood, such as being out for the count on Friday must mean that Saturday is pointless. It's not true. Add anxiety and the chemistry gets louder, cortisol narrows attention, and subtle positive signals don't get a look in.

Most poor decisions come from dodgy time travel and overconfident certainty. The antidote is boring and effective. Name your state before you prophesy. *"I'm tired. I'm wired. Then borrow one fact from outside the mood. Last time I felt like this and said yes, how did it go?"* If future-you at nine tonight wouldn't thank you, don't sell them your day. Use your best sleeping strategies, so that your *'Ah-Ha'* moment arrives in the calm mind, as the alternative of making a call with hot chemistry flowing through you brain, makes a very confident fool.

Then there's the intoxicating sense of rightness, that inner click that says, obviously I'm correct and only Muppets disagree. The delicious feeling to be right, terrible compass. The moment you stop allowing for the possibility that you could be wrong, your learning rate flatlines and your mistakes get expensive. Step out of the rightness room regularly. Ask, *'What would I see if I were wrong?'* Decide in advance how you'll know early if you've stuffed it.

Keep an eye on the usual suspects while you're at it. *Confirmation Bias, Availability Bias, Attribution Bias.* You won't delete them, but you can domesticate them, so when your limbic system puts on a high-vis vest and starts waving danger flags, delay the decision. Let your prefrontal cortex clock back on before you swing the hammer. This isn't about becoming robotic. It's about becoming trustworthy, to yourself and to the people who have to share rooms, projects, and kitchens with you. More prefrontal function gives you a clearer lens. A clearer lens leads to cleaner decisions. Cleaner decisions mean fewer heavy bags to carry.

Letting go isn't a talent you're born with. It's a practice, guided by a simple creed. *Don't carry what isn't mine. Don't cling to what isn't now. Don't confuse my feelings with the facts I still need to gather.* Looking differently is the companion skill. Assume the glass is smudged, clean it before you swear the view is broken.

Travel lighter. Look clearer. Keep your dignity. Keep your humour. The door's been open for years, so you don't need a new life to feel free, just a new way of carrying the one you've got.

9

Be The Architect Of Your Own Success

Reclaim power over your life and build a future not defined by chance.

WAITING FOR CONFIDENCE IS HOW PEOPLE STAY STUCK. It's understandable to hope the big break will wander up your driveway if you keep being decent and patient. We all know the stories about right place, right time, as if the Universe carries a clipboard and hands out tickets. Good on the lucky few. For the rest of us, waiting quietly for perfect conditions is a tidy way to lose a year. The truth is far less romantic and far more reliable. Opportunities don't simply arrive, they're built, piece by piece, while everyone else is refreshing their inbox.

No matter how many external forces try to push you, lasting change doesn't happen until you're internally ready to choose it. You might move because someone's on your back, and they might even claim a slice of the credit, let them. At the end of the day, it was still your decision. Change that sticks always belongs to the person who finally says, *'I'm doing this,'* and means it.

Taking charge begins with ownership. When you rely on luck, gatekeepers, or favourable winds, you park your future on someone else's property. When you act, you bring it back into your hands. That choice isn't loud or reckless, it's practical. It's about placing yourself in the path of possibility through small, repeatable behaviours that compound. The people you respect didn't float into position. They asked for the meeting, learnt the skill after dinner, showed up to small rooms and made them better. Ordinary beginnings, repeated, produced what now looks extraordinary.

Creating opportunity usually asks for three things working together. *Courage to step outside comfort. Creativity to imagine paths where none are obvious. Resilience to keep going when the first version flops.* In real life that looks like putting your hand up for a project that stretches you, asking one clean question in a room that prefers silence, sharing a small piece of work with someone you trust and asking for specific feedback. It looks like saying what you want out loud and backing it with behaviour that can be seen and measured.

Capability matters. Choose one skill that would genuinely improve your situation within three months and design a bare-bones plan to acquire it. Ten focused hours beats a dozen aimless articles. Put your hands on the tools, make the thing, ship it to a friendly audience, and ask for one improvement. Big enough to make you sweat, small enough to finish well.

Relationships create surface area for luck to land. Network intentionally, which is a fancy way of saying be useful, be curious, and be consistent. Turn up where your people actually gather. Follow up the same day with one sentence of thanks and one sentence of value. Keep a short ledger of who you learn from and what you can offer in return. Don't collect business cards, collect conversations you'd happily continue. People open doors for those who make rooms calmer and clearer.

This work doesn't just change your outcomes, it changes your interior. When you initiate instead of wait, you build self-respect, resourcefulness, and a steadier relationship with fear. Each time you start something, you send your nervous system a clear message. *I'm someone who can act.* That identity becomes a quiet engine. It hums under tough days and gets you moving when motivation goes missing.

Expect setbacks and treat them as information, not an indictment. If you're moving, you'll hear no, as you'll misread moments. You'll prepare well and still come second. Ask one short follow-up question, *'What would have made this a yes?'* Change one thing and try again somewhere else. Keep a pipeline rather than betting everything on a single golden ticket. Professionals make more attempts than amateurs and recover faster because they keep records of their tries instead of wounds.

Align your action with your values so you can keep going when applause is thin.

Write a small charter. *Here is the work I want more of. Here is how it helps real people. Here is the kind of person I want to be while I do it.* When you run your days from that charter, motivation becomes a choice rather than a mood, fulfilment follows because behaviour and belief finally match.

If you don't know where to begin, start small. Pick one area that needs a lift and take one step today. Momentum beats elegance every time. Small steps done daily will always outpace the perfect plan that never leaves your head.

Spend time with people who are building rather than complaining, their energy is contagious in the right way. Share intentions, not just outcomes. Ask what they tried, what failed, and what finally worked. Offer your own learnings in return, that shortens the distance between idea and execution and you stop talking yourself out of good work.

Keep a simple scoreboard. When the week feels flat, it will prove you're moving. When it lights up, let it count. Humility isn't pretending nothing happened, it's taking the right-sized nod and getting back to work.

A word on fear. It won't disappear because you were brave today, it will follow you into new rooms carrying a folder of your oldest mistakes. Thank it for the warning and give it a smaller job, it can check the exits while you speak. The only way fear learns its new role is by watching you act, as ten small actions teach it faster than one dramatic pep talk.

Making your own chances is less fireworks and more farming. You plant, you water, you tend, you harvest, then you start again. Some months the paddocks look bare. Keep turning up. Keep asking better questions. The satisfaction isn't that a break finally came. It's knowing you built a life where breaks keep coming because you learnt how to make them.

You can wait for the knock, or you can start knocking. Choice is written by your initiative, your courage, your wisdom and your decision to be the author of your life rather than the audience.

10

Deciding Isn't Doing?

What am I actually changing today? Where will it likely wobble? What will I do then?

TALKING ABOUT CHANGE FEELS PRODUCTIVE UNTIL life asks for action. Change has two speeds, *gunna do* and *doing it*, one makes speeches, the other moves furniture. If you're serious about real *Growth*, you'll need less declaration and more design structures that keep you honest on messy days when motivation forgets your address.

The first lever is how you tell the story of what's happening, it's the responsible narration where you're not denying reality, you're widening it so your nervous system has more than one exit. There are four moves that work reliably when the room tightens.

You reinterpret the event. That curt response to your *'hello'* first thing in the morning might not be contempt, it might be someone drowning inside whose attention has grabbed them and taken them sideways.

You normalise your biology. Of course you're rattled as your brain hates uncertainty and will treat the curt response as a threat until proven otherwise.

You reorder your values. Ask yourself whether you want to be right or effective, because those two don't always travel together, catch your threat response and determine if you want to be right or you can let it go and discuss later over coffee.

You reposition your view. Stand in the other person's shoes long enough to see a second angle, even if you don't adopt it.

***

Confidence gets talked about like it's a feeling, but most of the time it's choreography. One of the strongest humble little tools in our awareness tool box is called an *Implementation Intention*, if X happens, I'll do Y. That simple format builds a strong mental link, so when the situation appears, the behaviour fires without a pep talk or willpower arm-wrestle.

'I will eat better' lives in the never-never, contrasting to *'If it's 3:30 and I want sugar, I'll make tea and walk around the block once'* that actually lives in your body. Enough of these plans turn change into muscle memory. You stop debating your values and start behaving them, even when you're tired. Attention is the soldering iron that makes these plans stick, so when you focus deliberately while installing a new behaviour, you are literally wiring new circuits. That isn't mysticism. That's the brain doing what it does best, building roads where traffic keeps flowing. Short bursts of repeated focus, turns a dirt track into bitumen. After a month you're not trying to be different, you're simply acting differently.

Consistency is when your chemistry and psychology stop fighting and start pulling in the same direction. *Congruence* is when your goals stop sounding like slogans and start resembling your calendar. Both feel like better air in the room, not dramatic, just less friction. You'll know it's working when the two inner dials line up. This is where the *Impartial Spectator*, that calm observer who can see you from a slight distance without judgement or malice, earns its keep. When the day gets loud, invite them in. Ask, *'What's actually happening here?'* and, *'What would I advise if this wasn't my nervous system on the line?'* Name what's going on, *tight chest, story of disrespect, urge to fire back,* cools the limbic system and hands the wheel back to your prefrontal cortex (the rational front). Change is often nothing more glamorous than catching yourself before the old pattern drives again.

A word of caution though, not everything you face is a problem to solve as some things are polarities to manage, stability and flexibility, rest and effort, privacy and connection. Try to solve a polarity and you become rigid. Manage it with ranges instead. *'I train most mornings. I also sleep in after late nights.'* That maturity saves a lot of whiplash.

Change feels complex because it is. You've got billions of neurons in your brain firing through trillions of synapses, so with change you're asking a city to reroute traffic. The good news is *neuroplasticity* never clocks off and your *self-directed neuroplasticity* is simply you choosing which streets get the new bitumen. Repeat a path with attention and emotion and the map updates. You've felt the moment when a new behaviour stopped needing white knuckles and started carrying itself.

Your brain doesn't stop at your skull. Your gut and heart have their own networks talking to the limbic system all day. That's why disgust hits the stomach and heartbreak aches like a bruise. One of the fastest ways to prime change is movement as exercise releases the fertiliser neurons use to grow and connect. (Translation) Go for the walk as you're not just burning calories, you're greasing the rails for mood, learning, and memory. If you can, pair your new thinking with movement, the wiring goes in deeper, the tracks of change turn to roads and when you keep at it long enough you wont even notice the superhighway you've just built yourself.

However, expect resistance when you challenge the old map, for implicit memories run quietly in the background, efficient and automatic. They're why you can type, drive, and tie your shoes without thinking. When you ask for change, the *Amygdala* does its job and throws a flag of either fight, flight or freeze. That's not sabotage, its a speed bump. Slow the car, steer anyway as new doesn't mean unsafe, it means unfamiliar. Just keep going until the unfamiliar becomes ordinary.

There's a quiet power most people overlook, *Free-Won't.* Your free-will may be patchy, but your veto is strong. You may not summon the perfect response on cue, but you can delay (veto) the old one with a long inhale followed by a long ten second exhale. That gap matters, as saying *No* to your old reflex response is often enough and your *Yes* finally has room to land, that is your *Free-Won't.*

Change is slippery because habits and goals run on different tracks, one wants immediate payoff, the other cares about direction. Add *Cognitive Dissonance* to the mix and things get noisy. That's the grit you feel when what you do and what you believe start arguing in the same room. Your nervous system feels it before logic catches up, and the temptation is to rewrite the story instead of changing the behaviour. Knowing this helps as it turns self-judgement into strategy. Start where habits actually start, cues. Catch the cue and you can reroute the action.

When you feel hijacked, two moves help. Reappraise the moment (veto) where you become aware that this urge isn't a command, it's a wave, then label the feeling in plain language. Naming it drops the temperature and activates the brakes. That's wiring, not poetry.

After you choose differently a few times, confidence arrives quietly, not the chest-beating type, the evidence-based one. *'I did it. I can repeat it.'* That reward signal helps the brain take the win as normal, which is why a clean first week matters more than a dramatic first day.

Insight gets over-romanticised, as it is those sudden answers that usually arrive when the noise drops as it likes quiet corridors. If your mind is flickering, lower the load, Sleep, Rest, Healthy Food, Movement. Then ask again as often the solution was there all along, it just need some room amongst the mind full of noise.

If you want a simple way to bridge *gunna do* and *doing it* on an ordinary morning, try this. *'What am I changing today? Where will it wobble? What will I do then?'* Do the smallest honest version of your plan before lunch, then tonight, write two lines. *'What worked, and why.'* Then that becomes tomorrow's map. And, if you don't achieve you plan, rinse yourself of guilt, and repeat each day. Stack enough of those days together and people will stop hearing you talk about change, and start recognising you as someone who's doing it. No audition. No theatre. Just steady building.

11

Move or Stay Stuck

This isn't penance. It's a kindness with standards.

MOVEMENT ISN'T ABOUT FITNESS, it's about reminding your nervous system you're not trapped, as exercise is one of the most reliable contributors to personal *Growth*, and it's worth stripping it of all the nonsense so you can use it properly. Movement isn't punishment for eating, ageing, resting, or falling off the wagon. It's maintenance for being alive in a body. It keeps the wiring cleaner, the chemistry steadier, and the day easier to carry. You're not chasing aesthetics or redemption arcs here, you're building a body that lets you think more clearly, sleep more deeply, and respond to life without snapping at the first bit of friction.

The biology is straightforward and generous, when you move, your brain shifts chemistry in your favour. Brain chemicals, dopamine and endorphins lift your mood and motivation. Cortisol, the stress hormone that loves to linger when life gets loud, eases back. Blood flow improves, feeding oxygen and glucose to the parts of your brain that help you plan, regulate, and choose well. That's why a decent walk can untangle a problem that felt impossible on the couch. Aerobic movement for twenty to thirty minutes most days is enough to tilt the whole system, as anxiety loosens, stress falls, low mood often lightens. This isn't hype, its physiology doing what it's designed to do.

Movement also trains your nervous system to find rhythm again, as repetition builds predictability, and predictability lowers threat, so over time, your system learns that effort doesn't equal danger and exertion doesn't mean collapse. *Neuroplasticity* takes care of the rest, strengthening pathways that support focus, *Emotional Regulation*, and *Resilience.* (I'll give you the low down on them later) Add another human to the mix, once in a while, and your chemical soup improves again, because the brain links movement to connection and reward, that's why walking with a mate once a week often beats the most elegant solo program you never start.

The rule that saves most people is this, start where you are, not where you wish you were. If the last few years have been rough, illness, grief, burnout, then showing up is already a win. Think in terms of a Minimum Viable Session, ten to twenty minutes you can repeat even on your worst day. A brisk walk around the block, a simple strength circuit, push, hinge, squat, carry. Lifting groceries count, as does traversing up and down stairs. If you're already running or lifting, great, just don't idolise your best session and stall there. Train the body you have today, it's the only one available.

Make starting automatic by building cues into your day. Kettle boiling equals five squats. Lunch alarm is labelled WALK. Shoes live by the door so you trip over them. Hat by the keys. No Playlist so your head can clear itself, (that is, unless it's an audiobook of this Guide) Keep the mantra boring and effective. Same time, small steps, attendance first, intensity later. Consistency beats enthusiasm every time, because enthusiasm burns hot and disappears, while habits quietly carry you through the weeks that don't care how motivated you feel.

Cardio doesn't need drama to work as brisk walking is criminally underrated and wildly effective. Hills are a free upgrade if you want one, and if you hate running, don't run, pick the thing you'll actually do. Mobility deserves a mention too, especially if chairs are a close companion. Ankles, hips, thoracic spine, shoulders, two minutes each, most days, keeps the rust away and reduces the background aches that make people quit before they've begun.

If your life is packed, shift work, caring responsibilities, long days that don't respect schedules, then trim the program to fit the life rather than trying to force the life to fit the program. Keep a small go-bag in the car with shoes and a hat. Take the opportunities that appear, even if they're awkward. Ten minutes between errands still count. You're not training for the Olympics, you're training to be a human with a nervous system that behaves.

Bad days happen. When they do, use the two-day rule, never miss twice, and if yesterday fell apart, today doesn't need to be impressive, it just needs to exist. Ten minutes preserves the habit so tomorrow isn't a restart. On good days, resist the urge to empty the tank, leave a little in reserve, that restraint keeps you consistent and less injured, which is how you stay in the game long enough to get the real benefits.

Watch the way you talk to yourself about movement, as this is not a courtroom, it's a workshop. Fire the inner prosecutor who loves words like always, never, and useless. Bring in the inner manager instead. Short, civil instructions you can follow while tired. Shoes on, out the door, five minutes to warm up, one round to start. When the noise spikes, label it. *Heart fast. Jaw tight. Old story.* Then move your body for two minutes and see what's left as the brain believes the body more than it believes your speeches.

Community can help, but only if it matches your goals. One walking mate who keeps a steady pace is often better than a group that turns every session into a performance. Join a modest class if coaching keeps you honest. Or go solo with birds for company. Many people perform better in privacy. Know which one you are and stop apologising for it.

Protect the wins that never get posted. The commute you walk, the stairs you choose, the kettlebell you swing twice a week, the garden you keep alive. Remember that quiet pride beats loud misery as your body doesn't care who noticed, it cares that you showed up.

If your body has history, surgery, chronic pain, old injuries with opinions, you're not broken, you're experienced. Learn the difference between discomfort and pain. Discomfort is allowed and often required, pain that changes your movement is a stop sign. Adjust your range, slow the tempo, change the activity and be stubborn about the goal and flexible about the route. As water is your ally, so are physiotherapists and exercise physiologists who speak human and help you progress without bravado.

Fuel and sleep matter more than most plans admit. You can't out-train a fried nervous system so eat real (non-processed) food first and enough of it to support the work. Prioritise sleep because that's where repair happens and mood is set, and to complete the circle, movement improves sleep and sleep makes movement easier. That loop is worth protecting.

Tie movement into the rest of your life instead of treating it as a separate project. A walk becomes savouring when the phone stays home and the breeze gets your full attention. Lifting becomes gratitude when you thank past-you for laying out the gear. A cooldown becomes journalling when you jot one line. *What worked. Why. Next step.* You're building a web, not collecting hobbies, and each strand strengthens the others.

If numbers motivate you, keep a simple scoreboard. *Minutes moved, sessions done, steps climbed, mobility minutes completed.* Track outcomes too. *Mood steadier, sleep deeper, fewer arguments with self or others.* When the week feels flat, the scoreboard proves you're still moving. When it lights up, let it count, as humility isn't pretending nothing happened, it's taking the right-sized bow and showing up again.

Expect plateaus. They're not failure, they're information. Change one variable at a time. Add a hill, add a set alternate activity and if motivation dips, shorten the sessions and increase frequency as discipline grows when the habit is easy to start and awkward to skip.

If fear is hovering, give it a smaller job, it can check the exits while you walk. Nothing teaches fear its new place faster than you acting anyway. Ten minutes of movement will beat ten minutes of arguing with yourself every day of the week, and hold the tone as you go, this isn't penance, it's kindness with standards. Be decent to your body and ask a bit of it. Move first, talk later. If today is ten minutes, that counts, if you feel strong, don't waste it, either way, you'll be back tomorrow, same time, same shape. Not glamorous, but effective. That's how ordinary people get extraordinary returns, one honest session stacked on another until the day behaves better and the mind does too.

12

Choosing Your Guides Wisely

*The guides you choose will shape not just your direction but your character,
and the chemistry of your home.*

T HERE ARE SEASONS WHEN THE ROAD FORKS and the signposts blur. You stand there with a tight chest, three options, and a clock that refuses to slow down. In those moments it's wise to ask for guidance. The trick isn't just asking, it's choosing who gets to speak into your life. The wrong voice costs you time you don't get back, the right one saves you from avoidable detours and gives your courage somewhere solid to stand.

Here's a rule that sounds simple and keeps paying out. *Don't take guidance from people who are where you don't want to be.* Not because they're bad people but because most advice is autobiography. Most of us give directions from our own streets, we pass on the turns that got us here and quietly avoid the roads we were too afraid to take. If you don't want their destination, be careful taking their map.

Before you let someone steer, look at their life up close, not the brochure. Do their outcomes resemble a future you'd be proud to own? This isn't about being impressive, it's about being grounded. Look at the relationships that have survived proximity, listen to the tone they use on waitstaff, watch what they do when they've stuffed up. That tells you more than any highlight reel. If someone has trophies but no one in their house can relax around them, that's not a model for a steady life.

Values matter more than volume. Plenty of loud voices sound confident because they've never paid for their mistakes. The guides worth listening to can hold two ideas at once, ambition and decency, candour and care. They ask questions before they give answers, they talk about what worked and where it didn't. They don't recruit you into their identity war, they respect your pace and protect your privacy. When someone rushes you, isolates you, or shames you into agreement, that isn't guidance, that's control in a friendly disguise.

Your inner circle, *your tribe*, should be small and specific. Different lanes need different mentors. Take creative advice from people who actually make things and ship them. Take money advice from people who tell the truth about risk and still sleep at night. Take relationship advice from people whose loved ones would happily share a meal with them. It's fine to love your uncle and not let him near your finances. It's fine to admire a brilliant executive and not copy their eighty-hour week if you value a healthy home. Respect without imitation is a grown-up skill.

Family and friends usually mean well, familiarity, however, is not a qualification. Before you hand them the wheel, ask three quiet questions. Do they live by values I want to practice? Does their version of fulfilment look like mine? Do their results come with costs I'm willing to pay? If the answer's no, keep the love and limit the influence, thank them sincerely and steer by a different star.

Good guides share a few markers. They listen longer than they talk, they draw out your reasons before offering their own, they're suspicious of tidy certainty in complex situations. They talk trade-offs, not magic bullets, they help you clarify your direction rather than enrolling you in theirs. They don't need you to succeed in a way that flatters them. If they carry a bias, they name it. Humility isn't a vibe, it's behaviour that keeps your agency intact.

Red flags are just as consistent. *Absolute language. Gossip dressed up as insight. Urgency that makes you smaller. Secret rules that isolate you from other counsel. Promises of everything.* When you feel your world narrowing while they speak, step back. Wisdom widens your field, manipulation shrinks it.

Your role here isn't passive. Build an internal compass so you're not outsourcing your life to the loudest room. Get clear on the life you're trying to build and the person you're practicing becoming. Write it down where future panic can see it. When advice arrives, strain it through those filters, *'Does this move me toward the work, relationships, health, and peace I've named? If I follow this counsel for two years, who do I become?'* If your stomach hardens, *pay attention.* The body often spots a mismatch before logic catches up.

Test guidance small. Pilots don't leap from sitting in the cockpit to flight. They run checklists, they speak to the tower looking for clearance, they have a flight path and a working radar. You can do the same. Try the new behaviour for two weeks, measure real effects, not imagined ones, review your checklist. Debrief with someone steady, speak to your tower, keep what works follow your plan, and keep a check on your radar, it protects you from ideology dressed up as life advice.

Remember that seasons change. The mentor who got you moving may not be the one for maturity, the coach who helped you build boundaries might not be the one who helps you soften and trust again. Let roles evolve without turning people into heroes or villains. Thank them for the stretch of road they helped you walk, then adjust your advisory board as your life turns.

There's also value in learning from the negative. A chaotic boss teaches you how not to run a team, a friend who never apologises teaches you the social cost of refusing repair. You don't need to hate them to learn the lesson, you just need to say, that's not for me, and mean it.

Be careful with confidence, especially your own. If you've made a few pearlers in the past, you may be tempted to hand your judgement to anyone who sounds certain. Don't. Ask for examples, not slogans, ask for context, not commandments. Advice that survives questions is advice worth testing.

Keep your humour while you sort this out. You don't need to become the monk of discernment, smile at your habit of asking six people and then doing what you wanted anyway. Notice it. Clean it up. Make your circle smaller and your questions better. *'What am I missing? What cost am I not seeing? If this works, what new problems will it create?'* Good guides love those questions because they're building your engine, not just pointing down the road.

Be kind to the people who love you but aren't your guides. Most are trying to keep you safe with the tools they've got. Thank them and mean it. Then steer by your compass, as you can honour someone's heart without outsourcing your decisions to their fears. If they push, say it plain. *I respect your view. I'm heading a different direction.* That doesn't need a courtroom, it needs a steady voice and a short sentence.

If you want a clean way to start, try this for a month. Write the names of three people whose lives genuinely inspire you in the areas that matter. Ask each one clean question about a real decision you face. Listen for patterns. Test one piece of counsel. Debrief. Then send a thank you when it helps. Gratitude keeps the right people close.

The path ahead is yours. The guides you choose will shape not only your direction but your character, and the chemistry of your home. Choose carefully whose voice gets near the steering wheel. And when you find people who make you braver, steadier, and more honest, keep them close. They won't just show you the next turn, they'll help you become someone who can walk it well.

13

The Path That Shapes Us

Chaos to Coherence

WE WERE TAUGHT EARLY THAT LIFE SHOULD BE SMOOTH, that happiness follows a neat procession of milestones, and that if something barges into that parade and knocks a baton or two to the ground then we must have taken a wrong turn. We're handed a tidy map of how life is meant to unfold. Study hard, get a stable job, find the one, keep your head down, and somewhere along the way the pieces are supposed to click into place. Then real life turns up without asking for permission, bringing detours, redundancies, fallouts, medical scans, bills, and long nights that don't care how organised you were or how well you followed the instructions.

If you keep believing happiness lives on the other side of a cleared schedule, you'll spend years on hold listening to the same elevator music, waiting for conditions that never fully arrive. Life's challenges aren't detours from the path, they are the path, the path was never meant to be free of obstacles, the path *is* the obstacle. Who you become is shaped less by what happens to you and far more by how you walk through what happens.

So we learn to fear struggle and read it as failure, when in truth struggle is often the most honest thing in the room. What if struggle isn't the enemy at all? What if it's a guide? Once that truth drops out of theory and into your bones, you stop treating adversity like an administrative error and start meeting it as the very material you're meant to shape. The old, but true statement of '*What doesn't kill you, makes your stronger,*' fits right in here.

Setbacks are not verdicts on your character, they're invitations to grow capacity. A job loss can teach you the difference between identity and income. A breakup can show you where your boundaries were guessed instead of spoken. A health scare can stop you outsourcing your life to *later*. None of this is romantic, and none of it is punishment. It's simply the training ground that reveals strengths you didn't know you had because comfort never asked for them.

Growth, resilience, and insight are not delivered after a season of ease, they're forged in friction. In the phone call you didn't want to make, in the pay cut you didn't plan for, in the relationship that forced you to learn boundaries you'd been guessing at for years. Every obstacle, whether it's loud like a crisis or quiet like a persistent doubt, asks you to refine your character and clarify what actually matters. Not on the big days with witnesses, but on an ordinary one when nobody's clapping and you still choose to behave well.

There's a nervous system underneath all this philosophy. When the ground shifts, your body throws switches automatically. Heart rate climbs, breath shortens, vision narrows, and the clever part of your brain dims while the animal part takes the wheel. Don't treat that as failure. Treat it as a signal. First things first, drop your shoulders and lengthen the exhale. Put daylight on your face if you can. Drink water. Eat something real. These sound like small ideas for big problems, but they're scaffolds. Once the animal settles, the human comes back online. Then you can choose your next move instead of letting adrenaline choose it for you.

Waiting for perfect conditions robs you of the small miracles already happening. Happiness can live beside hardship, and often does. It turns up as a sunrise after a bad night. A mate sends a stupid meme at exactly the right minute. You finally finish a task you've been dodging and feel the quiet pride of having acted instead of avoided. When you register these moments on purpose, your mind learns to find light in dark rooms. *Savouring* isn't self-help fluff. It's how you file good experiences into memory so your brain can reach for them later, when the day tries to convince you nothing decent ever happens.

Presence doesn't need grand gestures or dramatic reinventions. It thrives on simple rituals that you actually repeat. A notebook by the bed with three lines at night about what the day tried to teach you. A short walk where the rectangle stays home and your eyes look far enough to widen your field. An honest conversation with one person who listens without turning your life into a panel show. A small act of kindness toward yourself that you do in public without apology, hand on chest, quiet words, you're doing your best in a hard hour. These things don't fix life. They fix your footing so you can meet life.

Modern culture sells a slick story that happiness equals ease and calm, which equals control, and if your life feels rough then something must be wrong with you. That story is seductive and completely unhelpful. It robs you of the richness found in difficulty, because discomfort is often the doorway to a more honest life. The tension you're resisting is usually the exact force pushing you to evolve, like a good coach who won't let you hide on the sideline and keeps pointing you back to the field. One more drill. One more honest rep. One more pass with your eyes open.

Adversity asks better questions than comfort ever will, and they're blunt. *Who are you when the plan collapses? What will you keep holding when your hands are full? What can you finally put down because you've carried it too long? What is worth defending and what is ready to be released?* Those answers rarely arrive on sunny days, they arrive when life strips away your protective stories and shows you how you really love, where you're strong, and where there's still work to do. It's humbling and, oddly, freeing.

Waiting for perfect before you allow yourself to live well is one of the great delays of personal peace as there is no perfect moment, for life is moving, unfinished, and unpredictable. Right inside that mess sits the invitation to practice presence, to notice small beauty, to take comfort in the ordinary, to stand with courage inside what is still unresolved. Living well doesn't require you to deny the hard parts, it asks that you don't let them swallow the whole sky.

Choosing this way of living takes intention, not the loud kind, the repeatable kind, where you show up again and again, even when it hurts. You build small rituals of reflection and gratitude that give your nervous system somewhere to land. You cultivate relationships that support rather than try to fix you, and you speak to yourself in a tone you'd actually use with someone you care about. Persistence here isn't perfection, it's staying present with what is, and trusting that it's enough to take the next decent step.

Underneath all of this sits a quieter shift, the movement from *Chaos to Coherence*. When you're merely surviving, life can slide toward chaos without asking permission, money gets noisy, health drifts, housing feels uncertain, motivation thins, relationships turn into loops of argument and repairs that don't quite hold. Over time that pressure can settle into deep unhappiness, even depression, without fixing the room you're living in. The aim of *Growth* in your life is not to eliminate difficulty, but to move from chaos toward coherence, from constant threat to steadier reward, from a life that frays to a life that holds.

I like the word COHERENCE because it spells out the qualities that turn a scrambling existence into one you can actually stand inside.

Connectedness: You're a social animal whether you like the label or not. Genuine connection with a few good people, your tribe, lowers threat chemistry and restores your sense of belonging. You don't need a crowd, you need two or three humans who can hold your truth and let you hold theirs.

Openness: Not the kind that spills your private life on cue, but the kind that keeps you honest with yourself and others. Open to feedback that stings but helps, open to new ways of thinking and being, as rigidity masquerades as strength until life asks you to bend and you snap.

Harmony: Isn't a mood, it's a design. Your calendar starts to resemble your values, work serves life instead of eating it, recovery is planned not accidental. Harmony isn't glamorous, it's how your hours are balanced so the important parts don't starve.

Engagement: You're involved in what lifts your tone, you show up in relationships, you give attention rather than handing it over to the scroll. Engagement doesn't mean frantic, it means presence.

Receptivity: Sounds soft but isn't. It's the strength to meet new ideas without folding your arms on reflex, it signals safety to others and calms your own system. It keeps you out of echo chambers.

Emergence: You begin to notice options where you once saw walls, you tell a better story with the same facts. This isn't spin, it's the discipline of asking what else might be true that would help you act with integrity today.

Noetic: Being aware of your knowing (inner-self), your conscious awareness of self, is your quiet identity. You know who you are and that you exist. You stop auditioning for roles you never wanted and start living the values you keep writing down. That steadiness has a way of calming rooms.

Compassion: Warmth on purpose, it starts with yourself, because if you can't offer clean kindness to yourself, you'll struggle to offer it to others. In practice it's tone, patience, and small acts done without witnesses.

Empathy: Feeling *with* others, staying connected whilst the others needs sit side by side with yours, rather than one on top of the other.

Running beneath all of this is your ability to regulate your emotional life on purpose. You won't always control how you feel, but you can choose how you respond. You adjust the dials through awareness, the company you keep, and the basics you repeat even when you're sick of hearing about them. Sleep matters. Food matters. Movement matters. They're not slogans, they're levers.

As you move from *Chaos* toward *Coherence*, the parts of your life stop pulling against each other and begin to pull in the same direction. Your sense of wellbeing lifts, and that steadiness spills into the lives of people around you in ways you may never see.

So here's where we land. The moments you were sure would break you often turn out to be the ones that built you into someone kinder and harder to knock over. When you stop resisting the hard parts of life and start walking them with presence, you begin to live properly. Not because everything is perfect, but because you're becoming whole.

Rituals of grounding work better than motivational speeches ever will. Ten minutes of stillness in the morning. A song that opens your chest instead of narrowing it. A shower treated like a reset rather than a rinse. The same park bench at lunch. The same cup of tea before bed. Call it boring if you like. Boring is repeatable. Repeatable becomes *Growth*.

Celebrate small wins before your inner critic edits them out. *Did you ring the doctor? Did you answer the hard email? Did you keep your voice clean in a room where the old version of you would've performed*? That counts. Put it in your ledger. Your brain respects evidence. Give it receipts for progress or it will keep issuing fines for crimes you didn't commit.

Your inner voice sets the tone for the entire walk. Speak to yourself like someone you're responsible for, not like a rival you're trying to beat or a client you're trying to impress. Support, not shame. The inner manager voice works best here. Short, clear, civil instructions. Shoes on. Out the door. Eat real food first. Wait twenty minutes before replying.

Stay connected. You don't climb well in a vacuum. A friend, a sibling, a counsellor, a mentor, you don't need a committee. You need one or two steady humans who can hold your story without trying to run it. Healing likes company. Wisdom often arrives wearing somebody else's boots, carrying soup, and refusing to let you talk about yourself like a lost cause.

Now for the mountain. Life is a trail with gentle slopes and ugly scrambles. Vistas arrive only after you've done the work. The steep sections are not proof you're lost, they're proof you're ascending to heights you haven't reached before. On the climb you'll question your footing, your plan, and sometimes your sanity. Good. Check your footing, then take the next step. Rest when you need to. Look back occasionally to see how far you've come. Most of us forget to do that. We remember the slip and erase the metres gained. Don't erase them. They're your competence made visible.

Let me ground this in a few ordinary scenes.

You look at your bank balance and shame starts constructing a character assassination. The old version spirals and buys something to feel better. The newer version names the feeling, calls the bank, writes a four-week plan, and tells one trusted person so you don't carry it alone. The number doesn't change today. Your direction does.

You sit in the driveway because the house is noisy and your chest is tighter than you like. The old version scrolls into a fog. The newer version breathes for a minute, chooses a tone, and walks in greeting the room with warmth anyway. You don't deny the feeling. You choose the behaviour. That choice becomes a habit. The habit becomes a home that's easier to live in.

You won't do this perfectly. You'll forget and go theatrical from time to time. You'll preach to yourself about your failings and then discover the sink is still full. Alright. The win isn't perfection, it's noticing sooner and returning faster. Repair what you nudged sideways. Offer one apology that counts. Put the phone in another room. Start again where you stand. You don't need to restart your life in the morning. You can restart by 3.10 pm.

There's a quiet power in staying the course without a parade. No one will clap you for choosing to be decent in private, and that's fine. Choose it anyway. Keep a few victories unadvertised so they can grow roots, the work you do off camera is the work you can rely on when things wobble. Showy strength often crumbles. Quiet strength tends to hold.

If your head keeps selling you the myth of the flawless path, retire it. No flawless path has ever taught anyone courage, patience, or grace under pressure. You get those in the rain, you get them on the days that ask for a version of you, you haven't met yet, that person arrives through practice, not miracles.

You're doing better than you think, not because life is easy, but because you're brave enough to live it anyway. Keep going, not toward perfection, but toward presence, toward the quiet confidence that even in a life that's never fully fixed, there is still so much worth savouring. Don't wait for everything to be okay before you begin to live well. Begin now, as you are, with the next small honest step you can stand by tomorrow morning for the journey you keep looking for is the one beneath your feet, struggles and all. Give it your full attention for one hour. That's how transformation happens, not in grand sweeps, but in ordinary minutes carried well. When the climb gets steep, remember why you started. Look up long enough to remember the view exists, then look down and place your foot. That's it. Again tomorrow.

14

Developing Meaning

You don't need to move country, change your name, or join an order.

W E SHOULD GIVE OUR LIVES MEANING by living in reality, in the now, not by endlessly circling the past or trying to outsmart a future that hasn't arrived yet. Meaning doesn't live in yesterday's regrets or tomorrow's predictions. It lives in what you choose to do with today, even when today feels small, ordinary, or heavy, especially then.

In the darkest seasons, meaning rarely shows up as a grand purpose, instead it shows up as one small thing you can still stand behind. One task. One person. One decision that says, this matters enough for me to show up. That single act, done honestly, becomes a foothold, tomorrow you find another, over time, those footholds turn into a path as it isn't discovered all at once, it's assembled, piece by unglamorous piece.

We get distracted by the idea that meaning should feel dramatic, a calling, a lightning strike. A moment where everything finally makes sense. That fantasy keeps people waiting instead of living, whereas real meaning is quieter and sturdier. It's the work you do even when no one's watching, it's the responsibility you carry well, it's the care you give when it would be easier to check out. It doesn't announce itself, it accumulates.

You don't find meaning by asking big abstract questions all day, you build it by answering small concrete ones. *'What needs doing here? Who needs me to be steady right now? What would make this moment more honest?'* When you stop chasing the perfect why and start doing the next right thing, the noise settles. You're no longer auditioning for a life, you're living one.

Start where you are, not where you wish you were as meaning grows in place. Learn your patch, your street, your people, your tribe, the rhythms of your days. Know the names that matter, notice the light, the weather, the small signs that tell you you're actually here. People who feel unmoored are often people who haven't landed anywhere yet. The benefits of orientation in your life is underrated, it anchors you.

Every life has some form of honest work in it, something that rewards attention and improves with practice. It doesn't have to be artistic or impressive, it just has to be real, converting attention into usefulness. Cooking, fixing, writing, teaching, building, organising, caring. It gives your effort somewhere to go. Twenty focused minutes on something tangible will do more for your sense of meaning than hours of abstract thinking.

Service matters too, and not the performative kind, the quiet kind where you lighten someone else's load without advertising it. You help because it's needed, not because it's visible. You'll notice something important when you do this. When your strength is placed under someone else's burden, your own worries shrink to a manageable size, they don't vanish, but they stop dominating the room.

Meaning also relies on rhythm, small repeated actions that say, *this is who I am and this is how I live.* The walk, the cup of tea, the phone turned face down at dinner, the line written in a notebook before sleep. These aren't habits for productivity, they're anchors. They carry you through the flat days when motivation disappears and discipline has to take the wheel.

Privacy plays a role here as well. Meaning does not need an audience, in fact, it often grows better without one. When every good thing is turned into content, it loses weight. Keep some efforts unshared, let them work on you instead of for you. Tell the people who need to know, let the rest notice the change in how you show up.

Boundaries protect meaning. If your days are filled with other people's urgency, there's no room left to live deliberately. Saying no isn't selfish, it's stewardship. You protect the hours that let you sleep, move, think, care, and create. Some people will resent that, that's fine, you're not here to manage others discomfort, you're here to live in a way that lasts.

Work doesn't have to be perfect to be meaningful. Some jobs are simply jobs, and dignity lives in how you do them. Younger people notice more than they admit as meaning often travels quietly through example.

Relationships carry meaning through reliability, not spectacle. Warmth, repair, speaking plainly, dropping scorekeeping, being someone others can relax around. If you're choosing a partner or close friend, choose someone you can be ordinary with for a long time, as ordinary is where most of life happens, ordinary is where meaning earns its keep.

Suffering complicates all of this, and pretending otherwise is dishonest. When pain is present, meaning becomes smaller and tougher, it looks like the walk to the letterbox, the appointment you keep, the paperwork you finish so tomorrow hurts less.. Meaning doesn't flinch from grief, it pulls up a chair and stays with the person who sits, not trying to fix you.

If you want a simple structure for a day with meaning, keep it modest. Wake and make the bed, not for discipline but as a signal that you're here. Touch daylight. Move your body enough to feel breath and blood. Do one thing that reduces future chaos. Put your hands on some form of craft, even badly. Help one person quietly. Eat real food. Step outside, without headphones, and notice something true. Say one decent boundary. Before sleep, write two lines, what mattered today, and why. Then rest on purpose.

Expect boredom. We've been trained to think meaning should feel exciting, it rarely does, it feels repetitive, sometimes dull, often satisfying only in hindsight. That's not a flaw, that's how foundations are laid, over time, days stop feeling random and start feeling like they belong to you.

Avoid two traps. Comparison and Fatalism. Comparing your life to someone else's highlight reel will either make you chase spectacle or give up entirely, both are dead ends. Fatalism whispers that it's too late or you've wasted too much time. Ignore it, as you don't need permission to begin again. You need one decision that honours tomorrow, made today.

Legacy isn't a plaque or a post, it's the tone you leave behind. The way people feel safer, steadier, or clearer because you were there. The standards you set quietly. The reliability others copy without ever saying so. You'll never see most of it. That's how you know it's real.

If this all feels obvious, good. Meaning isn't hidden knowledge as you already know how to do this. You've had days that mattered, the work now is to make them less accidental. Choose one habit that adds weight. One relationship to repair by one degree. One lie to stop telling yourself. Then repeat.

You don't need to escape your life to give it meaning, you need to arrive in it, for *'no matter where you go there you are.'* Wherever you are, and with what you have, live as if today matters, because it does to the people within reach, as their lives improve because you touched them.

15

Flow and Letting It Steady You

Practice being yourself, with both hands on the task and your attention where your feet are.

FLOW ISN'T MAGIC, IT'S MECHANICS, and once you understand the mechanics you stop waiting for the perfect mood and start creating the conditions where your mind naturally settles and locks onto something worth doing.

Flow is that state where you're so engaged in an activity that time goes quiet, your thoughts stop tripping over themselves, and you're in your own world in the best possible way, not escaping life, but stepping into a version of it where your attention isn't being yanked around like a dog on a short lead. Done properly, flow slows you down in the right place, stabilises your nervous system, clears the fog, and gives you the kind of insight you can't manufacture through overthinking.

The first truth is simple and slightly annoying, flow lives where skill meets challenge, which means it won't show up if the task is too easy or too hard. Too easy and you're bored and scrolling. Too hard and you're anxious and avoiding. The sweet spot is one click past comfortable, where you have to pay attention, but you're not drowning. That's why flow is common in things like music, sport, craft, writing, cooking, gardening, restoring an old bike, even cleaning a shed properly, because those activities can be tuned by tiny increments. A slightly harder chord change, a slightly longer run, a slightly cleaner cut, a slightly tighter paragraph. You don't need heroic difficulty. You need honest friction.

Now, the big reason most people don't get flow isn't lack of talent, it's lack of runway. They wait to feel ready, inspired, motivated, and that's backwards because motivation is a freeloader that turns up after you've started, not before. You want a simple runway that your nervous system trusts, and the easiest one is the 5–20–5 pattern, five minutes to enter, twenty minutes to work, five minutes to exit. The entry is just setting the scene so you can't wriggle out of it, clear the bench, open the file, sharpen the pencil, tune the guitar, lace the shoes, fill the water bottle. The work window is protected, no switching tasks, no *'just checking one thing,'* because that's how the rabbit hole opens. The exit is tidy and deliberate, write the next step, lay the tools out for tomorrow, leave yourself a marker so you can re-enter without negotiating with doubt.

Flow also hates an audience, and this matters more than people admit. If you're doing the activity while imagining how it'll look, how it'll be judged, or how you'll explain it, you've invited performance into the room, and performance makes you tense. Flow needs privacy, not secrecy, just freedom from being watched, including by your own inner critic. Put the phone in another room. Shut the door if you've got one. If you don't, shut the apps and shut the loop, and give yourself one clean rule, no decisions during the focus window, because decisions are trapdoors into distraction, and suddenly you're choosing playlists and fonts and reorganising drawers like that was the plan all along.

Pick an activity that actually absorbs you, not one that sounds impressive on paper. For some people it's drawing or painting, for others it's lap swimming, lifting, woodworking, baking, writing, photography, gardening, jigsaws, model building, coding, learning a language, even building a proper budget spreadsheet that finally tells the truth. The test is brutally practical. If the activity makes you forget your phone exists, it's a contender. If it keeps whispering *'check your messages'* every two minutes, it's not wrong forever, it's just wrong for today.

Expect the first week to feel messy. Your attention has been trained by dings and pings and little red dots designed to farm your focus, so when you try to concentrate your body will twitch like it's missing a limb. That's normal, you're not broken, you're rewiring. The fix isn't a motivational speech, it's containment, phone far enough away that getting it costs effort and a decision, tools laid out so starting is easy, timer set so your nervous system trusts the window, water nearby, chair comfortable, light decent. You're not trying to win a battle of willpower, you're designing a room where flow is the easiest option.

Once you hit flow, you'll notice the afterglow, and this is where the real value sits. Your heart rate steadies, your thoughts widen, problems that felt enormous shrink to their real size, and you start seeing the next sensible move rather than the dramatic one. That's why flow isn't indulgence, it's maintenance. It gives your system a daily reminder that you can hold attention, that you can build something, that you can finish a small piece of work and feel quietly competent, and competence is one of the cleanest antidepressants we've got.

If you've got a busy life, kids, care responsibilities, shift work, financial stress, your flow windows will be short and lumpy, so stop waiting for the mythical three-hour block. Think micro-flow, ten minutes while the kettle boils, fifteen minutes in the car before you walk into the noisy house, twenty minutes during a nap, and make the kit portable so you can grab it without fuss. A small note book and pen, sketch pad, skipping rope, pair of gloves and secateurs by the back step, text file called 'short bursts.' You're building islands of absorption in a busy sea, not relocating to Bali.

There's one more distinction that keeps you honest. Flow is not escape. If you're using the activity to avoid the hard conversation, the overdue appointment, the bill you've been dodging, then you're hiding, and hiding always charges interest. Flow is what steadies you so you can return to life and deal with it in good faith, so use it as a tool, do the scary task and then flow as a reward, or flow first so you enter the scary task with a calmer voice and a clearer head. Either way you're integrating, not disappearing.

Keep a simple record, not for ego, for calibration. One line per session, date, activity, minutes, how it felt, one learning. You're collecting evidence that you can concentrate and improve, and on days when your mood tries to sell you the lie that you never change, that ledger becomes receipts. You'll also notice something humbling and freeing, progress comes from small, boring sessions stacked like bricks, not from heroic binges that burn you out and leave you guilty for a week.

If you want a clean place to start, pick one activity and commit to twenty minutes a day for a week, same time if possible, same place if possible, and treat it like brushing your teeth, not like a personality statement. Lay the tools out the night before. Decide the smallest next piece of the work. Enter for five, work for twenty, exit for five. Leave a marker and come back tomorrow. That's how flow becomes a stabiliser rather than a once-a-month accident, and once it's a stabiliser your clarity improves, your decisions sharpen, and your life feels less like it's happening to you and more like you're actually in it, steering, building, and breathing properly again.

16

Your Brain Isn't the Boss

When in doubt, change your state before you change your story.

YOUR MIND IS MORE THAN THE WIRING OF YOUR BRAIN. If your brain and your mind were the same thing, a neurosurgeon could bolt in a new thought pattern like a muffler, send you home with a warranty card, and wish you luck at the next service, which is a deeply tempting fantasy, but unfortunately not how humans work.

Have you ever actually stopped to notice what you're carrying around all day, every day, without a manual, a charger, or a warranty card. Your mind. Not in a poetic way, but in a practical, almost absurd way. It's doing extraordinary work while you're making toast, driving to work, or lying awake at three in the morning negotiating with your ceiling. We rush past that fact because it's familiar, but familiar doesn't mean ordinary. Your mind is one of the most capable systems you'll ever own, and learning to understand it properly changes how you live inside yourself.

Before we go any further, we need to clear a common confusion, because it matters. Your brain is not your mind. Your brain is physical tissue. It lives inside your skull. It's biological hardware, alive, electrical, chemical, busy. It receives information through your senses, sight, sound, touch, smell, taste, and converts that incoming energy into signals. It stores memories. It regulates movement, breathing, heart rate, and a thousand background processes that keep you upright and breathing without you having to micromanage them. Your mind is something different. Your mind is what happens when that living tissue interacts with your body, your history, your relationships, and the world around you.

The mind is where thought, reasoning, meaning, emotion, and *Sentient Awareness* arise. Memories sit in the brain, but meaning is created in the mind. The brain records experience. The mind interprets it. The brain holds the data.

The mind decides what it means to you, how you feel about it, and what you do next.

Psychiatry Professor Dan Siegel wraps this idea in a sentence that can make your eyes glaze over if you let it, describing the mind as an *'embodied, relational, self-organising, emergent process that regulates energy and information flow'*, which is both accurate and spectacularly unhelpful until you translate it back into ordinary language. So let's do that, because this distinction matters more than it sounds like it should, especially if you're trying to change how you live rather than just how you think.

Embodied means your mind doesn't live only in your skull, it lives everywhere you do, which you already know if you've ever felt your stomach drop at bad news or warmth spread through your chest at a kind word. Your breath, your posture, your gut, your heart rate are not background extras, they vote on your mood all day long, quietly but persistently, which is why changing your breathing can change the channel your mind is on, not because of magic or willpower, but because the plumbing is connected whether you approve of it or not.

Relational means your mind is built in company, not in isolation, and you borrow and lend nervous systems constantly, often without a word being spoken. Sit near someone steady and your own system settles, sit near a human fire alarm and your shoulders creep up before you've had time to think. Your mind expects company and adjusts itself accordingly, and that's why presence matters more than advice.

Self-organising sounds impressive until you picture a flock of birds where no one is in charge and yet order appears as each bird adjusts to the next, because your mind works the same way. Thoughts, memories, body signals, the light in the room, yesterday's conversation, today's coffee all interact at once, and patterns emerge without anyone running the meeting, which is why you don't command your mind into order, you influence the conditions and let order form.

Emergent brings it home, because the mind isn't a thing you can point to, it's the pattern that arises when many parts interact, the way coffee and milk become something new once you stir. That's why there's no single lever to pull and no one cause to hunt down, and why small changes can ripple further than you expect when you give them time.

Energy and information flow is simply the traffic report. Sensations arrive as packets of energy, sight, sound, smell, touch, taste, your brain turns them into information through electro-chemical processes, and then sends instructions back out to the body and into your choices. Every sigh, every grin, every email you send is energy and information on the move, and when the flow is smooth you feel coherent, while when it jams you feel scrambled, irritable, or flat. Your job isn't to bully the brain, it's to tidy the flow.

A frame that often sticks is this. The brain is hardware, the mind is software, the body is the power supply and cooling system, relationships are the network, your attention is the cursor, and your inner manager is the user. When the screen freezes, yelling at the monitor rarely helps, so instead you manage heat, close a few tabs, check the connections, and reboot gently.

This matters because it gives you more levers than you've been led to believe. If the brain were the whole story, your options would be limited to pills and prayers, both useful at times but incomplete, whereas the mind is embodied and relational, you can shift it from the outside in. Walk and the mind follows, lengthen the exhale and the field widens, sit near someone steady and your system borrows their settings, because small moves create large effects when repeated consistently.

Someone always objects at this point and asks whether thoughts are just chemicals and electricity, and the honest answer is, sort of, because thoughts are what chemistry and electricity do when they run through a lifetime of pathways you've laid down. That's why the same trigger sends one person into gratitude and another into doomscrolling, and why neuroplasticity matters, because it tells us those paths can change through attention and repetition, which is why the tone of your self-talk matters more than a pep talk from a stranger. Your inner manager is teaching the brain where to lay the next walking track.

Where the mind *lives* has never been pinned down to a location, and that's fine. We don't need a postcode to know it's real. We know it by experience. As Descartes put it centuries ago, *'I think, therefore I am.'* Consciousness is your awareness of being alive, of existing, of being a sentient being, of having an inner life that no one else can fully access. That awareness is not a lump of tissue you can point to. It's a process, a living, changing field of experience. Inside that field exists an entire Universe, your thoughts, fears, humour, creativity, grief, hopes, memories, and private logic all coexist there, often arguing with each other like flatmates who never signed a lease.

Your mind processes vast amounts of information every second, most of it outside your conscious awareness, sorting, filtering, predicting, adjusting. It shapes how you see reality, how you read people, how you make decisions, and how you remember the past. No one else experiences the world exactly as you do, and that's not a flaw. It's the signature of your sentient awareness.

What often gets missed is how resilient this system is. Your mind adapts, it learns, it rewires. Even after trauma, loss, burnout, or long seasons of stress, it remains capable of change. Every challenge you've lived through has left marks, yes, but it has also built capacity and resilience. You didn't just survive events, your mind learned from them, sometimes clumsily, sometimes brilliantly, often without your permission. *Growth* doesn't mean nothing hurt, it means your system figured out how to keep going anyway.

Understanding your mind as something valuable also means taking responsibility for its care. A neglected mind doesn't break overnight, it frays over time, it becomes noisy, reactive, tired, and harsh. Self-care doesn't need to be mystical, it can be very ordinary. Quiet time without input. Writing things down so they stop circling the rumination. Breathing that actually finishes an exhale. Moments where you are not consuming the next goto thing. These aren't indulgences, they're maintenance for a complex system that's been running flat out for years.

Your mind also thrives on engagement, learning, curiosity, creativity, problem solving. When you stretch into new ideas or skills, you stimulate the brain and expand the mind's capacity to organise and adapt. A curious mind ages better, as you use it or lose it. You don't need to reinvent yourself, you just need to stay interested. Boredom isn't a moral failure, but chronic disengagement slowly dulls your sense of agency.

The stories you tell yourself matter more than most people admit, as your internal narration shapes your emotional world. If your mind keeps telling you that you're broken, behind, or incapable, your nervous system responds as if that's a threat and throws the limbic system (fight, flight, freeze) into overtime When you begin questioning those narratives, not with forced positivity, but with honest curiosity, something shifts. Ask one clean question, *'Is this story helping me move forward, or keeping me stuck?'* That question alone can change the tone of your inner life.

Though separate, your mind and body are close as siblings can get, they're in constant conversation as one informs the other. Stress shows up in muscles and your sleep, calm shows up in digestion and breath, movement improves thinking, rest improves emotional regulation. You cannot think your way into balance without involving the body. Likewise, caring for your body supports mental clarity, patience, and resilience. This isn't philosophy, it's physiology.

The people around you matter too. Minds don't grow well in hostile environments. Choose relationships that allow honesty without punishment, curiosity without ridicule, and rest without guilt. You don't need many in your tribe, just need a few who help your system settle rather than spike and offer conversation that feels safe enough to be real, is one of the most powerful mental health tools available.

When doubt or stress hits, remind yourself of this, struggle does not mean failure, it means your mind is responding to complexity. With time, support, and care, it can integrate those experiences into wisdom rather than scars. Healing isn't erasing the past, it's reorganising your relationship with it so it no longer runs your present.

Seeing your mind as something extraordinary changes how you treat it and you stop using it like a weapon against yourself and start treating it like a tool that deserves respect. You become more patient with your learning curve and more intentional about what you feed it.

Your mind is not just something you use, it's how you experience being alive. Honour it, look after it, work with it rather than against it. When you do, you don't become someone else, you become more fully yourself, steadier, clearer, and better equipped.

17

Awareness – Being Really Awake

Awareness grows with practice, not perfection.

NOW LET'S LIFT THE LID ON *AWARENESS* without turning it into a lecture you'd avoid before coffee. Think of awareness as the live feed of your life, the felt awareness of being you in this moment, noticing, choosing, remembering, and caring. It isn't the brain itself any more than a song is the guitar, because the brain is the instrument, astonishing and complicated, while awareness is the music that happens when that instrument is played in the room you live in, by the body you wear, with the history you carry, and the people and places that keep shaping you.

A useful way to picture it, is a stage and a spotlight where the stage is everything happening in and around you right now, the hum of the fridge, the pulse in your fingers, the thought about lunch, the text you still haven't answered, the unease behind your ribs you can't quite name. The spotlight is attention, and wherever attention points experience brightens and gains detail, while outside the beam there's still plenty going on, just dim and sketchy. Awareness is the scene that's lit, plus the quiet sense that you're the one holding the torch.

That spotlight isn't fixed. Under stress it narrows, gets jumpy, and flicks to anything that smells like threat, which isn't weakness but survival doing its job. When you're safe and resourced, the beam widens, allowing you to notice more, connect more, think in longer lines, and hold two truths at once. Training awareness isn't a fluffy side quest, it's learning to handle the torch so you can steer your day instead of being dragged by it, and *Mindfulness* is simply the skill of placing and keeping that beam where it helps, then returning it kindly when it wanders, which it will.

Awareness has layers, like the ocean. On the surface there's the immediate stream of sights, sounds, and sensations, beneath is the emotional weather that tints the water offering a background mood that makes a familiar street feel welcoming on the weekend and hostile during the week. And deeper again resides the storylines you've rehearsed for years, the rules you were handed, and the quiet contracts you signed to stay safe, loved, or useful. The brain supplies the chemistry and wiring that make those layers possible, but the experience of moving between them, catching yourself mid-script and choosing a different line, is your conscious mind doing what only it can do.

There's another distinction worth learning because it saves a lot of grief. The experiencing self is the part of you that lives events in real time, the taste of tea, the warmth of sun, the laugh you didn't expect, while the remembering self is the editor who later decides what the day meant, what to file as a win or a wound, and what to tell your partner over dinner. They don't always agree, and if you let the editor run unchallenged, it'll cut out every small good thing and stitch together a tale of failure, whereas conscious awareness lets you bring both to the same table and say, today felt heavy in parts and these three moments mattered, and both statements can stand.

Self-awareness is the next layer, awareness turned on itself, the moment you notice the pattern running you. You hear the tone you use when you're tired and change it, you spot the old story about never being ready and start anyway, you feel the spike of anger rising and keep your thumbs off the phone, which isn't magic but the simple gift of noticing before acting, the tiny gap where choice lives. If you want a practical way into that gap, label what's happening in plain words, *'I'm noticing tight jaw and fast breath, I'm noticing a story about being ignored'*. Language gives your system something to hold and often that's enough to put your steadier mind back in the driver's seat.

Your awareness attunes to other people like a radio locks onto a station, so sit near a steady nervous system and your own steadies, while walking into a room full of brittle sarcasm tightens your chest before you've said a word. This is why your presence matters more than your speeches, because the awareness you cultivate becomes a state others can borrow, and if you want to help a team, a family, or a friend in a rough patch, bring a larger, kinder awareness than the moment provides, keeping your voice low and clean and your face warm, which sounds small but is not.

We also need to talk about the narrator in your head, because it tries to pass itself off as awareness when it's really a running commentary. It can be helpful when factual and brief, but becomes a menace when it confuses volume with truth. Awareness lets you choose a different manager for that inner room, not a bully and not a cheer squad, but a decent manager who speaks in verbs and keeps you moving in small, sensible steps.

Where does all this meet the body? Everywhere. Awareness rides on biology, so poor sleep shortens the spotlight and makes it twitch, whilst food that loves you back widens the beam and a walk resets the beam faster than any pep talk. If you can't change your mind, change your posture, your breath, or your light, because your brain believes the body more than it believes your best intentions. Bring daylight to your eyes in the morning, breathe long on the exhale when the pressure rises, and move until your thoughts stop pretending to be emergencies, then choose again.

Awareness grows with practice, not perfection. You don't need incense or a mountain hut, just ordinary moments used well, feeling your feet while the kettle boils, pausing one breath before you check the phone, softening your eyes when a child is talking, or returning attention to what your hands are doing when you catch yourself rehearsing an argument with someone who isn't there. These tiny acts look trivial, but they are structural, because they lay a floor you can stand on when life throws a curve.

And yes, awareness has limits. Much of what you are, runs quietly in the background, habits, reflexes, old alarms doing their job to save energy and keep you alive, and the goal isn't to rip out the autopilot but to be awake for the parts that decide direction. You won't catch every pattern before it runs and you don't need to, because catching one, steering one, and letting the win count is enough, and tomorrow you'll catch another.

If you want a simple test for whether awareness is doing its proper work, look at the quality of your choices after a pause. Are they a little cleaner, is your tone a little kinder, did you move toward something that matters rather than away from a feeling, because if the answer is yes more often than no, your awareness is serving you, your people, and your purpose.

So no, the mind isn't just the brain in fancy dress. It's the living conversation between brain, body, and world, held together by the light of your sentient awareness. Learn to handle that light, point it where it helps, bring it back when it wanders, use it on yourself with decency, and offer it to others with care. Do that often enough and you'll feel the difference first in your chest, then in your calendar, and then in the way rooms settle when you walk in, because that's awareness doing what it's for, not a theory, but a way of being awake to your existence.

18

When Life Won't Slow Down - You Must

Let the runaway world keep running while you change your weather

IF THE WORLD KEEPS ACCELERATING, learning to slow yourself becomes an act of survival. Some people will tell you that modern life has smashed the old village to bits, that tradition has thinned out and we now live in a world where everyone knows everything and no one really knows anyone.

While that's not the full story, it's not wrong either. Sociologist Anthony Giddens sharpened the point when he described our time as a runaway world, moving faster than any era before it, broader in reach, and deep enough in its effects to unsettle the habits that once quietly organised our lives. You feel that speed before you've even had breakfast, when headlines line up in your mind like impatient children, when climate news sits beside mortgage rates, when wars flicker across a screen small enough to fit in your palm, and all of it lands in the same nervous system that still has to get people out the door and answer emails before nine.

Here's the part that matters more than we'd like. Even when global forces are bigger than any one of us, even when governments stall and systems grind along their own tracks, there remains a patch of ground that cannot be outsourced, the square metre around your feet and the circle of people close enough to hear your voice, your tribe. It's tempting to use the disorder of the world as a foundation for another wing of the Temple of Excuses, because if everything is chaos out there, then surely ducking, covering, and waiting for calmer weather is a reasonable response. Reasonable, yes. Useful, not often. *Growth* in your life is not built in committee rooms on the far side of the planet. It's built in kitchens, cars, break rooms, and backyards, in the ordinary places where choice still shows up each day with the same honest face.

You can blame traffic for your mood, your boss for your tone, your history for your habits, and it will all sound convincing enough late at night when the fridge light is doing most of the listening, yet the next morning the same decision will be waiting. Will you bring steadiness into the day or will you outsource it to circumstances? No one else gets to answer that for you, not your family, not your colleagues, not the neighbour who treats the recycling bin like abstract sculpture. It's confronting, and it's also the best news you'll hear all week, because it means the lever is still in your hands.

We live in a culture that loves experts, and with good reason, specialists save lives and build bridges that don't collapse, but the habit of outsourcing everything that hurts can quietly turn you into a passenger in your own story. Giddens noted our modern tendency to consult experts for general repairs and unexpected contingencies, and there's wisdom there, yet if that becomes permission to ignore what you already know, you're not being supported, you're being sidelined. You don't need a degree to notice that you're breathless after two stairs, that your temper arrives before your words, that your sleep is tangled and your breakfast comes wrapped in plastic. The obstacle isn't information, it's acceptance, because admitting you need your own help is harder than asking for anyone else's, and it ends the performance about why change is impossible.

If you refuse to help yourself, the people who love you will try for a while, and then they'll wear thin, and they should not have to carry a life you won't pick up. That's blunt, and it's meant to be, because there's mercy in plain talk. You are the expert on your own life, which doesn't mean walking alone, it means the manager is you. Others can encourage, check in, laugh with you when the plan goes sideways, and bring soup when things fall apart, but they cannot do the early nights, the honest conversations, the hard refusals, or the choice to put the bottle back in the cupboard. Evidence builds trust, and you need your own trust more than you need applause.

Of course there's fear. Leaving familiar patterns can feel like stepping off a well-worn path into scrub that rustles at the ankles. The routines you know, the dramas that spike your system in predictable ways, even the habits that exhaust you, all offer a strange kind of security, and walking away from them will light up your

Growth Without The Bullsh*t

alarms. Let it. Anxiety without a tiger is a body asking for reassurance, and reassurance doesn't come from argument, it comes from action. Keep today's change smaller than your excuses by putting daylight on your face early and drinking water before coffee. Speak one civil sentence where you used to throw a spark and go to bed earlier than your habit and guard that time like it matters, because it does. This isn't a moral project, its practical chemistry, and a rested brain is less theatrical and easier to live with.

You'll also be tempted to hide behind other people's opinions, because the Temple is rarely built alone. We gather like-minded mates who share our frame and baptise hesitation as caution and delay as wisdom, and while belonging matters, echo chambers don't help you move. Keep your close friends and then widen your tribe by one. Find someone who wants the best for you rather than the most from you, tell them the one change you're making this month, and give them permission to ask how it's going. You don't need a boot camp. You need a witness.

None of this denies the speed or scale of the world outside your front door. Globalisation doesn't ask for your consent and there's no opt-out clause for the risks that come with it. What remains true, though, is simple enough to live by. You act locally or you don't act at all. You choose the tone you bring into your home, the way you speak under pressure, the moment you step outside for air instead of scrolling yourself numb. Each time you do, you either add another room to the Temple, or you walk back across the street to the Café and order one change you can actually finish.

Call that move what it is, courage. You'll wobble at first. Old stories will dress up as logic and suggest a return to the familiar, just smile at them, thank them for keeping you safe when safety was the priority, and carry on. Fear doesn't vanish, it shrinks to fit the facts once your actions begin to stack up, and trust grows the same way, not through declarations but through repetition.

Yes, the world is fast, unpredictable, and sometimes unfair, and yes, the lever you hold is small, but it's yours, and there's more lift in it than you think. Take hold, move what you can, speak kindly and clearly, and let the runaway world keep running while you change the weather inside your own skin, because when you do that long enough, the people around you will feel it too.

81

19

The Tracks You Lay Down

Life takes shape, step by step, day by day.

EVERY HABIT LEAVES TRACKS, and sooner or later you have to walk them. The same machinery that builds good skills can also stamp in lousy ones, because if you repeat a thought often enough, even a cruel one, it starts to feel like truth. And if you act out a habit long enough your mind will keep running it like a favourite playlist, even when the song is wrecking your day, which can sound like bad news until you remember the door swings both ways.

Deliberate practice of better moves builds better wiring, and mindful attention, decent self-talk, and small goals you can actually hit aren't self-help slogans, they're the raw ingredients your brain uses to lay down stronger tracks than the old ones, so you don't erase history. You outgrow your history, not by pretending the past never happened, but by giving your system a better groove to follow, until it becomes the default.

This is the point where change often gets spooked, because entering a new world risks leaving behind what has felt safe for a long time, even if that safety came with a price tag, comfort foods, familiar routines, the road most travelled, and even the dramas you know how to survive can feel like soft furniture you can collapse into without thinking. Step away from that and anxiety arrives like a nervous relative who turns up uninvited, not because there's an actual physical threat, but because your mind has learned to treat the unknown as suspicious and the familiar as survival, which means internalised anxiety is often fear of what could be, including fear of positive change, because positive change still means change. When it rises, good intentions can get shoved into the background as your old system starts lobbying for the status quo, the framework of reality begins to feel shaky, the Temple starts to feel as if it might crumble, and your reflex is to run back inside and light a candle to Not Today, because at least Not Today is predictable.

When anxiety takes the wheel, it rarely drives alone, because negative self-talk climbs into the passenger seat and starts narrating the trip in the worst possible voice, and on cue you may find certain people around you pulling you back to their level, sometimes kindly, sometimes needily, sometimes with that old familiar tug that says don't grow, don't change, stay usable, stay small, stay the same person who makes our lives easier. This is known as *'crabs in the bucket'*, where just when you think you were clearing the top rim of the bucket, there is always someone ready to pull you back down to their level.

I'm not calling your friends and family villains, most of them are just running their own software and trying to feel safe in a world that doesn't sit still, but you do need to notice when an energy-sucking dynamic is trying to recruit you back into the old script, because it's very hard to build a new life while living inside someone else's comfort zone. The real skill here is learning to trust yourself enough to keep going even when your nerves are loud. Your progress doesn't require permission, and you don't have to win an argument with anyone in order to keep walking. Keep climbing out of the Bucket no matter how hard the crabs try to pull you back again.

A lot of this mess comes from a tidy myth we were sold early, that life should be smooth if you work hard, tick the boxes, find your person, and keep your head down. Then real life arrives and scatters the cones. Death in the family, redundancy, a diagnosis that changes the map, a relationship breakup that knocks the air out of you, and suddenly you're walking terrain you didn't choose. If you believe struggle means you took a wrong turn, then every hill feels like evidence you're failing. But here's the cleaner truth, the paths were never meant to be free of obstacles, they include them. Who you become is shaped by how you walk path, how you repair, how you keep your tone when you're tired, and how you choose your next step when the plan has fallen apart.

Waiting for perfect before you allow yourself any happiness is one of the cruellest tricks we play on ourselves, because perfect doesn't arrive, life is moving and unfinished and a bit messy by design. The longer you delay living until conditions meet your internal checklist, the longer you keep your own heart on hold. What changes things is the moment you stop treating difficulties as enemies and start treating them as part of the training, because resilience doesn't grow on a couch under perfect light, it shows up when the plan collapses and you choose to continue anyway. Courage isn't a speech, it's doing the next small right thing while your stomach is doing somersaults. Insight rarely arrives wrapped in a bow, it tends to knock on your door after a mess and ask whether you're ready to learn something you couldn't have learned any other way, which is why discomfort is often the start of a more honest track, and the very feeling you want to run from can be the nudge that says look here, grow here, set a fence here, soften here.

Picture your life as a trail, because it makes the point without drama, where some sections are friendly and some are a scramble, and you don't yell at the mountain, you climb it, slowing when you need to, resting without calling yourself weak, then standing and continuing. The summit isn't where struggle disappears, it's where you can finally see how every ugly step mattered, and you won't live at the top either, because life will ask you to keep walking, sometimes up, sometimes down, always learning, always carrying the change into the next stretch.

Your journey isn't private property either, it belongs to you first and it ripples outward into family, friends, colleagues, and community, because the way you regulate yourself, the way you repair after a mistake, the way you speak when you're tired, all of it affects the people within arm's reach. That isn't pressure to perform, it's motivation to practice, because when you strengthen your inner steadiness, everyone who sits at your table breathes a little easier, and that is one of the quiet ways *Growth* shows up, not as a grand purpose statement, but as the atmosphere you create.

A big part of building that steadiness is learning to guide your emotions on purpose, because *Emotional Regulation* isn't about being calm all the time, it's about having enough awareness to shift what you feel or how you respond rather than letting old automatic settings run the show. You're balancing threat and reward in your body and brain moment by moment, and it's never once and done, it's a set of dials you keep adjusting, so instead of waiting for the perfect mood, you learn the practical levers that move the system. Naming what you feel, even roughly, anger, loss, fear, can calm the machinery because it turns noise into signal, and then choosing one small action that helps rather than hurts, a breath that reaches the belly, a glass of water, a boundary you can say without a speech, gives the mind direction instead of spin. When stress narrows your vision, widen your field by looking far, stepping outside, letting your eyes take in the horizon and sky, because your nervous system follows your gaze and attention is the torch that decides what gets lit, and then ask a better question, not, *'Why am I like this?'* but, *'What would help by ten per cent?'* Because the mind respects useful.

Relationships regulate us as well, and you already know this in your bones, because you borrow calm from steady people and you borrow agitation from volatile ones, which is why your best self shows up more often when you spend time with people who can stay grounded without making a scene. Invest there. Hold close the ones who tell you the truth gently and can hear your truth without turning it into theatre, and offer the same back, because communities keep their chemistry healthy through that give and take, not through slogans and speeches.

Bring it back to repetition, because repetition is where change sticks and where people either quietly win or quietly drift, and the boring truth is that you practice the new moves until they stop feeling like pretend, you repeat better thoughts until they sound like your own voice, and you run the same small process on hard days and easy ones so your nervous system knows what to do when the weather turns. Notice what's happening, name it plainly, choose the next clean step, then move, because that little loop will get you out of more corners than any grand theory, and it'll do it without drama.

You will forget, you will slide into old grooves, you will declare yourself a lost cause yet still open your eyes next day, that isn't failure, it's a human system adjusting. So, the win is noticing sooner and returning faster, repair speed over perfection, restarting at two fifteen instead of writing the whole day off. You're not aiming for a spotless graph, you're growing a life that can be lived, which means the goal is consistency with compassion, not constant victory with a clenched jaw.

In the end, challenges don't block your path, they reveal it, because the moments you were sure would break you often become the ones that built you into someone steadier, kinder, and harder to knock over. When you stop treating the hard parts as an administrative error and start meeting them as part of the assignment, you begin your *Growth* journey. This takes time, it asks for patience, and it asks for attention tuned toward the good without denying reality, because you have more control over your next act than you think, and more control over the tone you use on yourself than you've been taught to claim.

So look down at the trail under your boots, because that's your life, not the imagined one waiting for perfect weather, this one, and you can walk it with presence, walk it with humour when you can, walk it with compassion when you can't, and when an idea from these pages circles back for the fifth time, you can smile, because that's your brain laying down a stronger track. Keep walking the same good ground until it carries you without effort, and change becomes second nature, because moving toward *Growth* takes shape the only way it ever does, step by step, day by day, in a body and a mind you're learning to steer with care.

20

Happiness Is Not Found, Its Trained

Your life is happening now! Not later. Not someday. Right now!

L ET ME START WITH A SIMPLE TRUTH, happiness doesn't arrive, it's
practiced in small, repeatable ways that saves a lot of wasted effort and a
fair amount of self-blame. Life will always contain problems, there will always
be something unresolved, something tugging quietly or loudly at the edges of
your peace, and that's not failure, it's the human condition doing exactly what it
has always done.

The real trap is postponement, the habit of telling yourself that once this settles,
once that gets fixed, once they change, then you'll finally relax and allow
yourself a measure of happiness. Well, you already know how that story ends.
The goalposts move, the list breeds, and your life sits patiently at the station
waiting for a train that never arrives.

Happiness often arrives in teaspoons at first. The warm mug in your hands, the
laugh you didn't expect, the quiet pride of keeping a small promise. If you notice
it and let it count, happiness grows like a muscle, not by ignoring pain, but by
sharing the space. Pain and happiness can sit at the same table without cancelling
each other out.

Happiness is not a jackpot that drops when the Universe finally reads your emails
and approves your application, it is a practice of small, deliberate moves done
with the lights on, fully aware that you are doing them, repeated often enough
that they turn into the quiet rituals that carry your day whether the weather
behaves or not.

At first this can feel staged and a little awkward, like learning a new gait after a
long limp. You notice a good moment on purpose, take a breath on purpose, offer
a smile on purpose. Give it a week and the staging becomes familiar, give it a

month and it is simply how you move through the world without needing a memo.

You are not an island either, because you are wired into other people at a biological level whether you signed up for that or not. *Mirror Neurons* light up when you see a face, a posture, a tone. Someone smiles and your circuitry warms, someone flinches and your body readies for impact. We catch feelings and we broadcast them too, which means happiness is not only about how you feel inside your own skin, its also about the emotional wake you leave behind and the one you choose to sail in.

You can watch this play out anywhere people gather. If you pay even casual awareness, observe that one irritable person can infect half a Café queue in under a minute, while a barista with a genuine smile and an unhurried tone can flip the chemistry of the room just as fast. None of this is mystical or sentimental, its wiring doing its job as your brain reads far more than words, the micro-movements around the eyes, the set of the shoulders, the rhythm and cadence of a voice. Without a single conversation we recognise tension, we recognise ease, and we adjust ourselves accordingly, often before we realise we have done it.

Empathy happens faster than thought, and the real skill is not drowning in it. If you work in human services, or in any role where people bring you their hardest days, you already know how easy it is to absorb other people's storms until you forget which weather is yours. Sit with sorrow long enough and your *Allostatic load* climbs, sleep thins, patience leaks, and burnout creeps in quietly, not because you are weak or insufficient, but because your biology has been overdrawn for too long. The answer is not to care less, which corrodes something important, it is to care wiser. That wiser care starts with awareness.

The brain carries a negativity bias for survival, which was brilliant in a cave and is less helpful in a calendar full of ordinary stressors. Guard your awareness like it pays the bills, because it does. Train yourself to notice the full scene, not just the lights and sirens. When a decent moment lands, savour it for ten honest seconds, eyes, ears, breath, the lot, because that brief pause stamps the circuit before *Hedonic Adaptation*, the mind's habit of quickly normalising gains and comforts, tosses the good into the bin marked ordinary. Then give yourself aftercare. Finish the shift, the visit, the hard conversation, and downshift on purpose, put daylight on your face, move your legs, drop your shoulders, lengthen the exhale. If a negative story is still stuck, do not take it home to breed, write ten lines no one else will ever see and close the book. Debrief with one decent human who speaks plainly and does not turn it into theatre. Rinse the day before you feed it to your family.

As you move through the world, bring warm eyes and a real smile from gate to gate, not forced cheer or brittle positivity, but real warmth with a posture that says you are safe with me. Let your voice act like a seatbelt, steady and protective, rather than a siren that spikes every nervous system in the room. Your own life may be messy, mine certainly can be, but you still own your face and your tone. Offer your regulated system to others for a few minutes and they will borrow it, and in that borrowing your own system steadies too. This is the clean loop happiness prefers, quiet, reciprocal, and remarkably effective.

Happiness grows best in unglamorous habits that would never make a highlight reel. Move your body most days, not to shrink yourself but to grease the rails of mood and memory. Pay attention on purpose, moment by moment. Choose small acts of connection. Learn a name. Send the message that says you were on my mind. Sit with your child for five minutes while they show you a world built from Lego and fierce conviction. Do one useful thing for someone with no invoice attached. Make something, a sentence, a sandwich, a cleared bench, a sketch of a plan. None of this needs an audience, for it will not trend anywhere except inside your own chest, which is exactly where it counts, because that quiet sense of honest contribution lifts your internal set point more reliably than applause ever does.

Happiness also needs fences, because *no* is not anti-social, it is how you keep *yes* warm. Protect the hours that grow your strength, sleep, movement, craft, time outside, honest conversation. You are not opting out of life, you are opting out of avoidable damage so you can show up where you matter. If you have lived with chronic worry or the habit of scanning for threat, happiness will feel suspicious at first, like a salesperson at the door with too much enthusiasm. Be suspicious, then try it anyway in centimetres. Anxiety is loud. Insight is quiet.

You do not beat your internal loud with being louder. Lower the volume of the body and the mind follows, through a longer exhale, eyes on the horizon, a steady walk until your breath reminds you that you are an animal, not an avatar.

Relationships are where happiness learns to walk. The tone you carry into a room raises or lowers the cognitive ceiling for everyone for people think better near a steady nervous system, children test fewer fences and partners unclench.

None of this is magic or moral superiority. It is a brain no longer spending its daily budget on defence, for other people's brains work better when you broadcast warmth and clear intent, and your own day gets easier as a result, which is happiness doing practical, unromantic work.

When happiness remains partly yours, it can do its deeper work without being chewed by opinion. Tell a person, not a platform, and keep some victories unadvertised, not every good thing needs an audience. On the days that are genuinely heavy, grief in the house, pain in the body, chaos at work, aim smaller than happiness. Aim for steadiness. Aim to not make it worse. Sometimes the bravest thing you will do is take your own hand off your throat, as self-respect is not a prize at the end of the road, it is the tone you use at the beginning, and that tone is the floor happiness stands on.

If your work exposes you to heavy stories, build decompression into the job rather than treating it as an optional extra. Five quiet minutes of deliberate breathing before you drive home, music that widens the chest, a regular conversation with someone who can say you are carrying more than you think and mean it. Protect days off that are actually off, because recovery that never quite happens becomes exhaustion wearing a brave face.

Happiness without meaning feels thin and brittle. *Growth* is enhanced when you carry weight that matters and carry it cleanly, it shows up in being useful to real people rather than impressive to imaginary ones, service does not require a photo, for the craft of *Growth* is practiced without a parade. Place happiness on that foundation and it stops floating away, and yes, some days you will miss all of this and go full goblin, doomscrolling, sarcasm, biscuits for dinner, convinced civilisation is hanging by a thread and that thread is your inbox. Fine. The win is noticing sooner and returning without drama. The mind does not care about speeches, it cares about the next act.

Do not wait for the storm to pass before you feel the rain on your skin. Take the smallest honest piece of beauty available and let it count. You will forget, you will get theatrical, you will declare your life on hold until everything behaves. Notice sooner, return sooner. Start with the next five minutes, one decent thing for your body, one kind thing for someone else, one small order brought to one small corner of your world.

If you want a pocket line to carry this week, try this, *be the person who improves the chemistry of the room.* Do it with steadiness, with a face that says safe here. Do it with a tone that does not spike. You will feel it first in your own chest, then in the way people stop bracing when you walk in. That's happiness doing its proper work, not a high, a habit, not a mood, a method. It's available right now and it belongs inside a life, not parked at the end of it.

21

What You Focus On Becomes Your Life

Be present. Be kind. Be real.

A TTENTION, WHEREVER YOU POINT IT, LIFE FOLLOWS, and that's not mysticism dressed up as wisdom, it's mechanics playing out quietly and relentlessly. Where attention goes, energy flows, and what flows repeatedly through attention quite literally sculpts the brain's wiring over time, it's not about forcing better thoughts, but about developing better aim. When you learn to catch yourself in the act of noticing rather than being dragged along by it, you stop letting the day drive you like a stolen car and start taking responsibility for where you are actually headed.

American Journalist and Author Elizabeth Gilbert once described what Buddhists call the *Monkey Mind*, that restless, swinging bundle of thoughts that leaps from limb to limb, scratching, howling, grabbing at whatever shines next, and most of us recognise it instantly because our own minds behave the same way. Thoughts ricochet through time, half weather report, half gossip column, replaying yesterday, rehearsing tomorrow, rarely staying where your feet are. You were trained at school to think, solve, plan, rehearse, and strategise, all useful skills, but almost no-one taught you how to be aware while thinking, how to notice the thinker rather than being owned by it. The monkey ends up running the switchboard. You can start with breakfast in the kitchen and arrive at work at lunchtime with no memory of how you burned three hours.

Attention and *Awareness* are cousins. Awareness is the moment you say, I'm here, and then ask, what now, because without that pause you're not choosing, you're just momentum wearing a watch. Attention is how we navigate life. A good navigator checks the instrument panel as well as the horizon, but most of us drift, and then one day look around and say, I never meant to end up in this job, this suburb, this mood. Of course you didn't. That's what drifting does. It moves you somewhere technically reachable and emotionally confusing. You've met the autopilot version of yourself when you've driven through lights and roundabouts and suddenly found yourself outside work with no clear memory of the journey.

That isn't possession or a glitch, its attention siphoned off by preoccupation, usually the sticky, trivial stuff that feels important until it isn't. Meanwhile your working memory, think of it as the brain's Random Access Memory, (RAM), fills with half-thoughts, slows down, and starts throwing a little beachball of indecision, leaving you wondering why basic choices feel like wading through porridge. When the RAM is jammed, emotions run hot, judgement runs cold, and small problems dress up as big ones. This *'Allostatic Load.'*

There's an extra cost most people don't see coming. Mind-wandering doesn't just correlate with unhappiness, it actively helps create it, not because imagination is a flaw, but because repetitive, aimless wandering pulls you out of your own life and makes you oddly unavailable to the person in front of you. You can feel it in relationships when responses sharpen, listening thins, and warmth gets rationed. Attention isn't a mood, it's a stance, paying attention on purpose, in the present, without turning into your own judge and jury.

The present moment is all you actually have. One minute ago is gone. One minute from now hasn't happened. Planning is useful as long as you don't expect it to arrive on schedule, and catastrophising is pointless because it tries to live tomorrow with today's emotions. Much of our misery comes from two old habits, clinging to a golden past or running from a painful one, plus a future forecast that insists on dragging the nervous system forward into trouble that hasn't arrived. If you insist on living in the future, congratulations, you're already there, it's called *now*, for the reality pill will continue to highlight to you that, *wherever you go, there you are!*

In many Asian languages, heart and mind are not enemies, they are the same word, and that matters. When attention teams up with kindness, seeing gets clearer. Your mind becomes a sixth sense among the others rather than a tyrant perched above them, which is the flavour of attention that actually sticks, warm-eyed instead of cold, curious instead of clinical.

***

Meditation, stripped of incense and mystique, is simply the push-up of attention, the practice of being a human being rather than a human doing. You can sit, stand, or walk, the posture matters far less than the tone. You have your choice of meditation music, it doesn't matter if its Ohm, waterfalls or rainstorms, or better still go for a walk, take the ear pods out and notice the birds, the trees, sun on your face, the shape of the clouds. No matter the meditation road you take you'll still notice the mind wandering, accept it as normal and move on to gently escorting it back to the centre, without insults, without theatre, just notice and return. That's it. You are building a muscle you can use everywhere else, and this matters because you need a steady inner manager issuing clean, workable instructions. The aim is recalibration, not confession.

What keeps derailing us are the same three drivers playing dress-ups, grasping, aversion, and delusion. Grasping grabs because it feels incomplete. Aversion flares because something isn't how you want it to be. Delusion spins a story and then prosecutes anyone who disagrees. Attention doesn't eliminate these forces, it keeps them on a short lead. You learn to give them a seat, and then you can make a decent decision instead of a dramatic one. Attention is not the breath, the sound, or the thought, it is the knowing of those things, that objects come and go, knowing remains.

When you practice, you're not trying for perfection, you're stabilising the knower, which is why small, frequent pockets of attention change you more than rare, heroic sessions ever will. Ten honest seconds at the sink, water on skin, jaw unclenched, that's you touching base with reality before the inbox tries to tell you who you are.

Certain attitudes make this easier, you suspend judgement long enough to report honestly before evaluating. You practice patience, letting things unfold on their own clock, because hurry is an efficient way to miss the only moment you can act in, *now*. You meet the scene with a beginner's mind, allowing yourself to be surprised even when you think you already know. You trust your basic decency and the simple rule to do no harm. You accept what is here so the next move can be wise, because refusing reality burns the only fuel you have. You loosen your grip on storylines that keep you stuck, and in doing so free your hands to do something useful.

You will forget all of this repeatedly before lunch, and that's fine. The win is noticing sooner and returning without theatrics. Be your own decent companion. Ask better questions, keep your humour handy, because the monkey mind hates being laughed at and loses half its power the second you smile and say, *'Alright champ, back on the mat.'*

When life gets loud, two anchors help more than most advice. The first is breath and body, a longer exhale, a softened jaw, feet felt on the floor, crude and effective, because the brain believes the body more than it believes speeches. The second is clean edges to the day. Start with a clear aim and protect the first few minutes from screens, and at night give yourself space before bed so the mind can settle without being dragged through other people's noise.

As long as you're breathing, there is more right with you than wrong, and that the next decent moment isn't hiding behind a paywall or waiting for conditions to improve. It's here, under your nose, waiting for you to show up. Be present, be kind, be real. That's how you stop being dragged through a day you barely remember.

22

Freedom Starts the Moment You Stop Avoiding

Freedom awaits you, not through the absence of fear but through your courageous willingness to embrace it.

THE DOOR YOU KEEP WALKING PAST IS USUALLY THE ONE that opens your life. Many people keep their heads down, keep things smooth, and quietly hope that peace will arrive if they can just step neatly around life's uncertainties. That instinct makes sense because we are wired for safety, predictability, and the promise that freedom lives somewhere inside a well-padded comfort zone. The trouble is that real freedom, the deep and durable kind that still holds when the weather turns rough, rarely grows in padded rooms.

You will always have problems, and there will always be conflict humming somewhere in the background of a real life, that's not a personal failure, it is the entry price. The skill is learning how to let freedom exist inside the day while you solve what needs solving, which is not denial or naïveté, it is maturity. If you wait for a perfect forecast before you allow yourself to breathe, you will hold your breath for years and call it patience.

There is an old line worth keeping close, that *the secret freedom is courage,* and it deserves to be read slowly because it tells the truth without decoration. To live with genuine fulfilment, you need to feel free to make choices that align with who you are, and that kind of freedom is not just the absence of external rules or pressures. It is the steady unhooking from the internal ones, the fears, insecurities, and inherited expectations that keep you performing someone else's script long after the audience has stopped watching.

Courage is not the absence of fear, it is the recognition of fear combined with the decision to move anyway, because nerves are a normal response whenever you contemplate change or challenge a story you have carried for years. What separates people who live courageously is not a special gene or unusual confidence, it is a habit of action, because every time you do one honest thing while afraid, you quietly push the fence posts of your life outward, freedom expands a little, as a by-product rather than a chase.

Most of the barriers to freedom do not live out there in the world, they live between our ears in tidy narratives about who we should be, how we are meant to behave, and what other people might approve of or withdraw from. Some of those stories help us act with integrity, but many of them are cages built to please a past audience, and courage asks us to test the locks. It invites us to say, I am allowed to redefine my life based on honest needs and values, even if that makes some people uncomfortable for a while, which is not rebellion for its own sake, but adult responsibility for your one life.

If you think back to your truest moments of freedom, you will probably notice that they arrived when you acted from the centre of who you are rather than from fear or obligation. You told the truth and discovered the relationship could hold it. You tried the thing you secretly wanted to try and found you were more capable than you had been led to believe. You changed direction and felt your shoulders drop almost overnight. Those moments are not accidents, they are the natural side effects of freedom meeting courage.

Courage is a skill, not a stunt, and like any skill it grows through repetition rather than grand gestures. Start small and name one area where you feel restricted, then ask yourself what you are actually afraid of and what one step is small enough to do today and real enough to matter. Have the ten-minute conversation you have been avoiding. Send the polite no without an essay attached. Share the song, the sketch, or the rough draft with one person you trust. You do not need to lift the world, you just need to keep showing up.

Who you surround yourself with, you tribe, matters more than most people like to admit. Choose people who value your honest *Growth* over your old performance, people you can share dreams, doubts, and half-formed ideas with without being laughed back into your box. A good tribe does not pressure you to conform to their comfort, they remind you who you are when you forget and nudge you forward when you stall. If someone only cheers when you stay small, that is not support, it is a preference, and you are allowed to choose differently.

Setbacks deserve plain language too, because courage does not promise a smooth run, it equips you to handle the bumps without becoming them. You will misread a situation and overstep. You will undercook a plan and need to recalibrate. Treat these moments as tuition rather than identity, ask what the event is trying to teach you, adjust one behaviour, and take the next step while the lesson is still warm. People who live courageously are not unscathed, they are simply quicker to repair and slower to dramatise.

There is a quiet discipline that keeps courage alive in everyday life. Telling the truth, especially to yourself, and keeping small promises that only you will notice. Protecting your mornings from noise so decisions come from intention rather than panic. Moving your body so your brain remembers it is not trapped. These are not heroic acts, but they lower the cost of doing the right thing, which makes courage more available on ordinary days.

Some days your courage will be visible, standing up for someone who is being steamrolled, or owning an idea no one else wants to be seen carrying. Other days your courage will be private and just as real, sitting with an uncomfortable feeling without numbing it, resting when your ego demands grinding, or choosing not to re-enter a conversation that always ends in the same ditch. As you practice, notice what freedom feels like in your body, because there is a physical signature to living aligned, a looseness in the jaw, more depth in the breath, a wider angle on the moment, and that sensation can become a reliable compass.

Some people will misread your courage as defiance or ego, because they preferred the version of you who kept the peace at your own expense. Be kind and firm anyway. You are not responsible for protecting other people from the discomfort of your *Growth*, you are responsible for living a life you can stand in. Over time your steadiness will speak for itself, and the relationships that matter will adjust, because real freedom does not arrive when uncertainty disappears, it arrives when you decide to live freely in its presence.

Courage gives you permission to choose what is aligned, to explore work that fits your hands, to love without performance, and to build relationships on truth rather than appeasement. Freedom then does what freedom always does, it gives you room to breathe, to recover, to contribute, and to savour the ordinary splendour of a day that finally feels like yours.

So keep going. Do not wait for fear to vacate the building, walk with it and shorten its leash. Take one decent step, then another. Speak one clean sentence, then a second. When you wobble, recover. When you win, let it count. This is how courage compounds into freedom, and how freedom opens a door that lasts, not because life got easy, but because you stopped hiding from the life you were meant to live.

23

Hope – Optimism - Moving Forward

You're not auditioning for a different personality, you're building a different day.

HOPE ISN'T A FEELING, IT'S BEHAVIOUR that keeps moving when motivation disappears, and it's not a mood you wait around for like better weather, it is a method you practice, and *Optimism* is not pretending the tide has already turned, it is deciding how you will row while you wait for it to change.

When I talk about *Hope* here, I am talking about something practical and grounded, a clear goal, at least two honest pathways, and the willingness to keep moving when plan A collapses like a cheap deckchair. When I talk about optimism, I am talking about the tone of your inner voice while you work that plan, steady, clean, and untheatrical, because life will remain life, messy, late, and occasionally unfair, and we do not bargain with that reality, we build a way through it that preserves dignity and momentum.

Most people have been sold two poor substitutes. The first is toxic positivity, the idea that if you just smile harder, manifest harder, and deny the storm long enough it will turn into sunshine, which is not hope at all, it is performance. The second is smart cynicism, very fashionable, very clever, and absolutely useless when the lights go out. Real optimism does not deny pain and it does not worship it either, it names the weather and chooses a route. *'This is hard, and here is my next honest move,'* is a sentence that will carry you further than a thousand motivational posters ever could.

Hope weakens when the horizon gets too big. People do not lose hope because they are lazy, they lose it because they try to fix a year in one pass. Do not do that. Shrink the field. Pick one outcome for the next twenty-four to seventy-two hours that you can actually influence, write the smallest repeatable step, and do it before lunch. Hope grows where agency lives, and agency lives inside small, controllable actions taken now, not in speeches about later. Then give every goal two pathways, because when plan A jams, plan B keeps you moving. If the gym is packed, use the park. If the call is not returned, write the letter you will hand over when the time comes. If it pours, walk in a coat. If your energy is a puddle, halve the task and finish it tomorrow. This is not lowering standards, it is refusing to let one closed door turn into a closed day. Hopelessness loves all-or-nothing thinking. Hope loves options.

Language matters here, so speak behaviours in the present tense, *I train at five. I log off at six. I return calls within the hour. I cook on Sunday.* This is optimism as a contract rather than a vibe, and it works because your mind recognises choreography. When the sentence describes an action, the body knows what to do next. Keep the instructions clean and uncomplicated so you do not lose momentum in negotiation.

Evidence beats affirmation every time. At the end of the day, write two lines only, what worked and why it worked, not feelings but facts. *Better mood because I walked early. Cleaner meeting because I brought the numbers. No blow-up because I paused for ten seconds.* When you can link cause to effect, you begin to predict your own wins, and that prediction becomes the backbone of optimism. It is not, *everything will be fine*, it's, *if I repeat this, tomorrow improves by five per cent,* and five per cent compounded becomes a very different life.

You cannot stay optimistic on a diet of doomscrolling and gossip, so protect the first ten minutes of your morning and the last thirty minutes of your night from your phone, because that alone restores agency. Replace one feed with one real thing, like a page of this Guide, a walk without headphones, three handwritten lines about what you will move today. You are not going monk, you are going selective, and optimism requires attention, which is not a renewable resource when every app is trying to farm it.

On crisis days, shrink optimism to the next two hours. Big plans are brittle when you are raw. Ask what would make the next two hours survivable and slightly proud, then do one of those things. A shower. A call to the GP. Eggs on toast. A bill paid. A room aired. A walk around the block. A lie-down with the window open. This is not being small, it is being precise, for optimism is built like scaffolding around a damaged building, slowly and section by section, until the structure can carry itself.

Optimism has a close cousin called *Expectation Management*. If you keep handing your hope to people who have shown you they will drop it, you will end up jaded and loud. Honour reality, believe patterns more than promises, offer second chances with boundaries. You are allowed to protect your optimism from serial vandalism, because forgiveness can coexist with distance.

You do not need to narrate your rebuild to strangers, in fact, secrecy often keeps optimism alive in its early stages. Plant the seed in quiet soil, let the roots take hold, and when the first shoots appear, share carefully with people who want the best for you rather than the most from you. External applause is a sugar hit. Internal credibility is food.

Your nervous system responds better to ceremonies than to grand rituals, small repeatable signals that prove you are someone who begins again. The same mug at the same table, shoes by the door, a journal open on the bench with the pen already waiting. These are not cute details, they are instructions to the body. People who feel optimistic are not lucky, they are ritualised, having removed fifty decisions from their mornings and left only the ones that matter.

Do not confuse optimism with speed, for some repairs take months and some futures arrive quietly. You will not always get the montage, however you will get repetition. Repetition can feel dull up close, which is fine, because boredom is often where the future hides. Keep laying planks, the call, the walk, the meal, the boundary, the paragraph, the invoice, the stretch, lights out. The day may tell you nothing is moving. Your ledger will say otherwise. Trust the ledger.

Humour helps, especially the kind that loosens the jaw and lets air back into the room. Laugh at the drama you nearly invited in, at the grand plan that fell apart because you forgot your wallet. Hope loves humility, because humility can learn and grandiosity cannot. Be willing to be the student of your own life, because it is the only course that never stops paying you back.

If you are carrying grief or long illness, you are not excluded from hope, you are often its most disciplined practitioner. Yours may sound quieter, slower, and less impressed by shine. It may look like kindness in a waiting room, a walk to the letterbox, a well-timed nap, a hand held, paperwork handled so tomorrow is gentler. Hope does not bully you for not bouncing, it sits beside you and says, we will do what we can today, and that will be enough.

Pair hope and optimism with the body by moving first and thinking second. A brisk walk stabilises chemistry better than a pep talk. Simple, non-processed, food at regular hours does more for decision-making than any clever thread. Sleep on purpose beats ten mindset hacks. This is not anti-mind, it is pro-physics, because you cannot think well in a body running on fumes.

Finally, protect the tone. Speak to yourself like a competent adult you are responsible for, without tantrums, flattery, or cheap shots, and issue clean instructions you can follow. Shoes on. Out the door. Send the email. Call the friend. Cook the thing. Breathe. Hope and optimism live in those sentences because they arrive when you carry them out. You are not auditioning for a new personality, you are building a different day.

When doubt starts heckling, give it a job, guard the boundary rather than drive the car. That is hope and optimism in practice, and you may be surprised by how ordinary the bridge felt while you were building it, and how strong it is now that you need it.

24

Stop Living Like Everything's a Threat

A meaningful life, in a more sustainable way.

J UST AS THE ANIMAL BRAIN IS WIRED TO SPOT A PREDATOR, your social brain is wired to scan for dangers that threaten its core concerns. Before your brain can do its higher functions it runs an old organising principle that kept your ancestors alive, minimise danger and maximise reward.

You can see this in a simple bushwalk moment. You are strolling along a dirt track, sun on your skin, mind half on the scenery and half on nothing much, and then you freeze because a shape ahead looks like a snake, and without asking permission your system stops you in your tracks, heart and muscles ready, breath held, attention narrowed. A few seconds later your senses fill in the missing detail, you bend down and pick up a stick, and the whole body does that slightly embarrassed reset where it pretends nothing happened. That is not you being dramatic, that is your brain doing its job. The same machinery shows up when you meet someone for the first time and you get that odd internal tug that something is not quite right, a little *avoid this* signal before you can logically explain it. People call it a gut feeling. Treat it as information, not a verdict, because it is often your social brain noticing patterns faster than your polite brain can translate them into words.

Now take that predator wiring and place it in modern life, where the predators are not teeth and claws but criticism, exclusion, uncertainty, humiliation, and unfairness, and you start to understand why one sharp email can ruin a perfectly good morning.

Our desire for approval from a loved one, mate, or colleague, and our need to belong to a group, club, team, workplace, your tribe, is not vanity, it is your brain trying to maximise reward through connection, recognition, and safety in numbers. We love to be loved, seen, and appreciated, and when we get that reward the brain pays us in chemistry that opens the gates for learning, creativity, patience, and decent behaviour. When that reward goes missing, when you are iced out of the chat, talked over in a meeting, ghosted by a friend, or made to feel like an inconvenient extra in someone else's story, the minimise danger setting kicks in and you feel threatened, rejected, flat, or oddly angry. Some people go loud and prickly while others go quiet and disappear. Either way performance drops, not because you suddenly became useless, but because your biology is busy protecting your *tribe belonging ticket*.

Here is the part most people feel but do not name, social pain. It recruits some of the same neural circuitry that handles physical pain, which is why rejection can feel like a punch you cannot point to on the body and why our language borrows physical words to describe it. That overlap does not mean rejection is identical to a broken bone, it means your brain treats social threat as survival relevant. You are not soft. You are wired.

The social brain is not your enemy either, it's an old watchdog doing its best. If you give it signals it understands, clear rules, earned respect, honest choice, warm connection, and fair play, it settles, and when it settles your intelligence returns, your humour returns, your creativity stops hiding under the bed, and you are much more likely to behave like the person you actually want to be. The world will still get prickly because people are people, but you will have a plan that does not depend on everyone liking you on cue. That's not just neuroscience, that's plain old fashioned dignity.

Everyone has certain domains that light up when they feel threat or reward, and if one or more of those domains gets jabbed you can become harder to communicate with and nearly impossible to connect with in a calm way. While if those domains are respected you open up, you listen better, you speak better, and relationships get easier. The trick is not to pretend you are above this. The trick is to have a few predetermined responses so you can *respond* rather than *react*, because overreacting creates more threat and underreacting usually turns into a slow simmer that leaks out sideways later.

This is where Australian Neuroscientist David Rock's SCARF model earns its keep. SCARF is not a personality quiz or corporate decoration. It is a user manual for social chemistry, five levers the brain cares about so much it will happily swap IQ points to protect them. When one of these feels threatened, your system does not ask permission, it pulls the fire alarm. When one of these feels respected, your shoulders drop, your thinking widens, and you become the useful version of yourself you actually like. Think of SCARF as the rules of the room inside your head that minimise danger and maximise reward. You cannot turn the rules off, but you can know them, and knowing them gives you choice.

Status comes first because we all pretend we do not care about it when we absolutely do. Status is not peacocking. It is the basic question, *'Am I being respected here?'* Your brain answers before you have finished your coffee. A sideways comment in a meeting, a partner's eye roll, a child ignoring you for the dog, these land as drops in rank the nervous system wants to fix immediately. That fix might look like sulking, spiking, explaining too much, or going silent, depending on your style, but the underlying drive is the same, restore respect, restore safety. The irony is that scrambling to look important usually makes you less effective. Status stabilises when your contribution is real and repeated, not performed, which is why the quiet competent person with clean follow through ends up setting the tone while the loudest unit slowly runs out of oxygen.

Certainty is next because your brain is a prediction machine that prefers any map to none. Take away the map and it will draw one in crayon on the nearest wall. That is why ambiguous messages feel like personal attacks and why waiting for results can turn grown adults into twitchy meteorologists. The point is not to demand a life without uncertainty, that is fantasy and property brochures. The point is to notice how much calmer you become when you can see the next anchor point, what is happening next, who is doing it, and when we will talk again. It is mostly logistics, not poetry, and it works because the nervous system loves a simple sequence.

Autonomy is the right to steer your own trolley. It is not rebellion. It is oxygen. When people feel trapped, even good people become strangely oppositional, and you can watch it happen in workplaces, families, and committees where someone loses choice and suddenly starts fighting over the smallest things as a way to reclaim control. Autonomy does not require grand gestures. It often looks like being allowed to solve a problem your way, or being given options instead of orders, and those tiny freedoms tell the nervous system you are not cornered. Funny thing, when people feel they can choose, they cooperate more, and when they cannot, they comply until they find a window to undermine the whole process.

Relatedness is the *us* button. Your system is forever sorting people into safe, watch, and do not engage without biscuits, and the body relaxes in the presence of *us-ness*, shared effort, warm tone, and small signals that you matter. You do not need a tribe of thousands. A handful will do if they want the best for you, not the most from you. You already know the feeling. In certain company you think better, your jokes grow up, your courage expands a size, and that's not magic. That's a nervous system no longer spending half its budget on defence.

Fairness is the quiet judge. It stays silent until it has been ignored for a while, then it brings the whole tent down. Unfairness is rocket fuel for anger because it whispers, *'You are not safe here, the rules cannot be trusted,'* and we notice it in pay, praise, speaking time, invisible labour, and the little exceptions handed to favourites. The grown up response to unfairness does not require a placard. Mostly it is clear standards applied the same way each time, transparent decisions, and the willingness to fix crooked systems without a speech about how hard it is to be fair. People can handle tough outcomes if the process is clean. What they struggle to forgive is being spun.

Here is the kicker. All five SCARF levers fire the same survival chemistry, because your body does not differentiate much between a dent in status and an actual tiger. Social threat steals resources from your clever brain to fund your survival brain. That is why you can walk out of a curt meeting and forget your own phone number, yet leave a generous conversation and produce your best idea before the lift dings. Brilliance is not only a trait, it is a state your body either permits or vetoes depending on the social weather.

SCARF also explains some of your so-called mystery moods. If you ever felt rattled after a conversation that was not objectively terrible, run the SCARF scan.

Maybe you were dismissed or interrupted *(Status)*. Maybe the plan kept changing *(Certainty)*. Maybe your method was overridden *(Autonomy)*. Maybe the vibe was cliquey *(Relatedness)*. Maybe the rules bent for someone with louder shoes *(Fairness)*. Naming the lever lowers the temperature because you stop fighting ghosts and start asking better questions. *'What exactly are we deciding and by when?'* restores certainty, *'Can I run this my way if I hit the outcome?'* restores autonomy, *'Can we make the standard consistent?'* restores fairness. The chest loosens, the thinking returns, you are back in the driver's seat.

This model works at home as much as work because partners do not argue about dishes, they argue about fairness and status, and kids rarely melt down solely because of bedtime, they melt down because autonomy got ripped away in one grab and their system went to war. It can sound exhausting to name it all, but you do not have to analyse every moment like a lab tech. You just make small humane adjustments. A clearer map here, a bit more say there, a nod to effort without a song and dance, a repair when you misstep. The atmosphere changes, people stop bracing and start behaving.

Leadership, big or small, is mostly SCARF management with manners. The best leaders I have seen, Parents, Coaches, Sergeants, Nurse Unit Managers, Board Chairs who are not addicted to their own voice, all do the same quiet things. *They explain the why so certainty is not a rumour, they politely ask for input early so status is not a competition, they give autonomy over method so adults feel like adults, they build relatedness without turning work into a cult, they treat fairness like hygiene, not a quarterly keynote.* The result is not a cult of personality, it is a room where people can think.

There is also a personal angle you cannot ignore. Your self-talk is either a SCARF stabiliser or a threat amplifier, as the inner voice that sneers *idiot* is a status punch. The one that says *'I never know what I am doing,'* demolishes certainty. The one that orders you around like a prison guard shreds autonomy. The spool that says *'everyone else has it together,'* knocks relatedness and fairness off the shelf in one swipe. You don't need to become a cheer squad leader, but you do need an internal manager, brief, factual, and decent. *'Alright, here is what we know. Here is what is next. Here is where you have a choice. You have handled worse with less.'* That tone will not trend online, but it will get you through the day with your dignity intact.

SCARF also explains why privacy feels medicinal. If every move is open to *'comments, likes'*, then status and fairness are permanently up for public auction, certainty changes with the crowd, autonomy becomes a poll, and relatedness turns into performance. No wonder you feel cooked. Keep some wins unadvertised, let your nervous system have a room where it can work without being watched.

Humour helps as well, when it is kind. A wry line at your own expense lowers status anxiety in the room. A joke about the plan that you thought would take twenty minutes and ate the whole morning before lunch, gives everyone certainty that you are still human. A light quip about choosing the left fork this time nods to autonomy. A shared laugh is relatedness in shorthand. If you can smile and say, *'Alright, even the dog can see that wasn't fair,'* without venom, fairness gets a chance to stand up without a fistfight. Wit that does not require a victim is leadership on a plate.

You do not have to memorise SCARF or tattoo it somewhere regrettable, just carry the idea that your brain is a social organ trying to keep you alive with people. It is not weak for caring, it is wired. When you stop treating your reactions as moral verdicts and start reading them as signals, you get choice back, and you can decide to take a breath before you bite, ask a clearer question before you spiral, invite a quieter voice before the loud ones set the agenda.

Most of us will not redesign a company or a country, but we do design rooms every day, kitchen tables, Zoom/Teams calls, school runs, committee meetings, Friday drinks, and that quiet bench outside the servo where a mate tells you something that makes your chest ache. In those rooms your SCARF is either being yanked or gently adjusted. Pay attention to the hands near it, including your own. Keep it warm, keep it decent and watch how much smarter, kinder, and braver people become when the levers are set close to humane. And once you know which levers have been pulled, you need a simple way to self-regulate so you can *respond* rather than *react*, because this is where the real win lives, not in never being triggered, but in recovering faster and choosing cleaner.

Start by labelling what is happening in plain language, because naming a state gives you a little control back, and it helps you spot personal biases, group dynamics, or old sensitivities that might be inflating the moment. Then get curious, because *'that's interesting'* is a surprisingly powerful circuit breaker when your system wants to go to war, and curiosity makes room for options. Next, explore which domain is being threatened. *'Is this status? Is this certainty? Is this autonomy? Is this relatedness? Is this fairness?'* Then reappraise by asking whether there is another way to view the situation, what is the opportunity here, what can I learn, and what is the smallest adjustment that would turn this into something useful.

Learn the SCARF domains not only for how you treat people, but for how you recognise which of your own levers has been bumped by others, because that awareness is what allows you to intentionally regulate your emotions and keep your behaviour from doing damage you later have to clean up. Do that consistently and you will notice something quietly powerful, not every discomfort is danger, and treating it that way shrinks your world. Your relationships become easier to maintain, your work becomes less exhausting, and your days stop being run by invisible social alarms, which is a very practical kind of freedom.

25

Updating Your Inner GPS

Refuse to let yesterday's template drive today.

WHAT GOT YOU HERE WON'T GET YOU where you're meant to go next. Your brain isn't just a social organ, it's a navigation system with opinions, and when life has been shaped by trauma, addiction, burnout, grief, or long seasons of survival, that navigation system becomes jumpy, reactive, and overly protective. In those states, relationships tend to poke every alarm you've got, not because the people in your life are the problem, but because your system is running old threat software on new terrain. If you want those bonds to survive and even deepen, you can't live on reflex alone.

You have to learn to think about your thinking, not in a navel-gazing way, but like a pilot glancing at the instruments before committing to a landing. The academic term for this is *Metacognition*, but all it really means is noticing the story your mind is serving, checking the settings, and updating the map before you drive it into a ditch.

Your brain receives energy from the world whilst your mind actively re-creates it. Culture, history, attachment, and the people who shaped you all feed into what neuroscientists call a *Re-entry Loop*, the repeating cycle where experience becomes interpretation, interpretation becomes wiring, and wiring steers the interpretation of the next experience. These loops are made up of networks of cortical firing, streets that light up together like a city map at night, with the *Prefrontal Cortex* acting as air-traffic control, coordinating what gets priority and what waits. Every glance, tone, text message, memory, and sigh is energy and information entering that system. That's why a casual remark from a partner can knock you sideways, because your brain didn't just hear a sentence, it activated an entire suburb of old streets, producing that familiar, *'Where did that come from?'* feeling.

Here's the catch. We don't share the same maps, even though we talk as if we do. We assume our meanings are obvious, our reactions reasonable, and our interpretations universal. They're not. Each person is navigating with a customised map built from their facts, their assumptions, their earlier conclusions, and the emotional weather present when those conclusions were formed.

Two people can witness the same event and chart entirely different routes to safety, then argue as if one of them must be lying, when in fact both are navigating faithfully according to their own cartography. Your GPS is not the only authorised edition to recognise that emotion acts like a highlighter pen, the stronger the feeling, the deeper the memory embeds itself in the network. That's helpful when learning not to touch a hot stove, but far less helpful when a raised voice now equals danger simply because once, long ago, it did.

Over time, these emotionally charged memories turn into trust maps, who feels safe, what tone signals care, and which tone means brace yourself. With repetition, the map gets paved in asphalt, fast and automatic, until it starts to feel like reality rather than a draft. This happens through a simple but sneaky chain, you receive information, accurate or patchy, you draw assumptions, sensible or wild, you rely on conclusions you made before the facts even arrived. You layer interpretations, yours and other people's, on top, then you add the energy of the moment, whether you were calm, hungry, embarrassed, or exhausted, that emotional voltage can turn a clear map into a labyrinth. Two people can hear the same five words and, depending on that voltage, one feels supported while the other feels hunted. If you want relationships that don't detonate, you have to factor emotional charge into your reading.

This is where *Attentional Intelligence* earns its keep. When you pay close attention, the kind that truly locks onto the person or task in front of you, different regions of the brain synchronise into a larger working circuit. Often you'll feel it as a small internal click, the moment confusion relaxes into clarity. Attention literally rewires which streets are available to you. The challenge is getting enough of it online to interrupt the re-entry loop before it drags you down an old road at full speed.

Put this in everyday terms. Your partner sighs when you walk into the room, old map says, sigh equals rejection, prepare defence. New map pauses and checks instruments, maybe they're tired, maybe work was a circus, maybe they're thinking about the price of groceries. That sigh may have nothing to do with you. Attentional intelligence is the ability to say, *'Hold, don't guess,'* while you gather one or two pieces of fresh data. The old map will still offer last year's route, you thank it for the warning and ask for an update.

Of course, you won't always manage this gracefully. Sometimes you'll snap first and interpret second, because you're human, not a robot in sandals. It isn't about perfection, it's about swapping old templates for fresher interpretations more often than not. That requires humility and practice, the willingness to admit your map is a draft rather and the discipline of keeping the prefrontal cortex in the pilot's seat when emotion tries to hijack the plane.

It also helps to learn your personal glitch points, the cues that reliably light up your threat board, such as delayed replies, changed plans, or a particular tone. Label them. The brain settles when it knows what it's dealing with. Then, when the cue appears, you don't need to perform surgery, you just need to keep your hands off the siren long enough to collect one more fact. Relationships improve dramatically when two adults can say, *'This is where my map goes funny,'* without demanding the other person change the weather to suit.

On the other side of the table, accept that your partner, friend, or colleague carries wiring built from different storms. You don't have to adopt their map, but you do need to respect that it exists. If you want to function well together, as partners, co-parents, teammates, or friends, you build bridges between maps. Shared definitions, predictable rhythms, and a few clear rules that protect dignity when everyone is tired. That isn't control, it's mercy, and it gives both nervous systems something solid to lean on while you sort out the rest.

You'll hear plenty about living in the *now*. Practically, that means updating the map in real time. You notice when you're navigating with a detour designed for a decade ago, and ask one clarifying question before launching the artillery. You remember that the aim isn't to be right, it's to be reliable. Reliability means your behaviour is increasingly guided by present cues and chosen values, not by old alarms demanding tribute.

Two truths are worth keeping close. First, attention is finite, if you hand it to every ping, you won't have enough left for the person you're trying to love. Protect it like a scarce resource because insight prefers quiet corridors, and most arguments can wait ten breaths. Second, maps change fastest in respectful environments and minds relax where status is acknowledged, certainty isn't a rumour, autonomy isn't stripped away, relatedness is genuine, and fairness is consistent. In other words, social weather matters. You think better in some company, so choose that company, your tribe, when you can and help create it when you can't. It isn't about becoming a saint with a permanent calm smile, it's about becoming a decent navigator with honest instruments.

You'll still take wrong turns, everyone does. The win is noticing sooner, turning gently, and refusing to let yesterday's template drive today into a wall. Keep your sense of humour, keep your dignity, and keep updating the map. The people walking beside you will feel the difference long before you do, and one morning you'll realise you're on a genuinely new road, not the old one with better signage.

26

Meeting Yourself In The Shadows

You are not running anymore. You are meeting yourself, and you are bringing yourself home.

RUNNING AWAY FROM PAIN OR HIDING FROM DIFFICULT truths has a funny habit of bringing you back to the same place. The route might change, the scenery might look new, and the cast of characters may rotate, yet the feeling waits patiently at the next stop, tapping its foot like it always knew you'd arrive eventually.

We all carry an inner world with us, made up of memories, beliefs, fears, hopes, and half-finished feelings that never quite got a proper ending. You can change jobs, move house, swap friendship circles, clean up your digital life, and still find that your inner world rides shotgun, *'Wherever you go, there you are.'* That can sound discouraging until you see it clearly, because if the baggage is always with you, then freedom was never about running in the first place. The baggage doesn't fall off when ignored it just gets louder.

Think of it this way. Hold a glass of water in your outstretched arm and it feels easy enough. Hold it there for a minute and it's still manageable. Hold it for five minutes and your arm starts to ache, your shoulder complains, and before long the shaking begins. The weight of the glass hasn't changed. What changed is how long you held it. Most of what exhausts us in life isn't the issue itself, it's the prolonged effort of avoiding, suppressing, or carrying it alone.

Freedom begins when you turn toward yourself with curiosity, kindness, and courage. You stop sprinting past the dark hallways in your own house and instead pick up a lantern and walk into those bits that were never brought fully into the light of conscious life. Unfinished conversations, unresolved hurts, choices you regret, and moments where you did the best you could with what you had. When you approach these without judgement, something shifts. Past experience turns into information. Information turns into choice. Choice turns into change.

Presence is the practical skill that makes this possible, it means anchoring your awareness in what is actually happening now, including the parts you'd rather avoid. When anxiety or regret whispers, *'get me out of here,'* try staying, not forever, just for a minute. Pause and notice the urge to flee. Name what's here, even roughly. *'This is sadness. This is anger. This is shame.'* Then offer yourself the tone you'd use with someone you love. *'I see you're hurting. I'm here.'* From there, get curious and ask what this feeling might be pointing toward. You don't need an essay, for often the first honest answer is enough to steer today by a degree or two.

These small moments of presence add up. Each time you stay with yourself for sixty seconds instead of bolting, trust grows. Over time, you become someone you can rely on when the room gets loud. You stop needing to fix everything before you breathe, because you breathe first, then decide the next small move. That order matters more than most people realise.

Meeting your shadows isn't meant to be a solo expedition. You're allowed to have company, people who can hold a torch when your own light feels thin. One steady friend who listens like an adult. A family member who knows the unpolished version of you. A counsellor who speaks human rather than theory. Let them sit beside you without turning your story into a spectacle. Reflection helps too. Journalling gives shape to feelings that otherwise blur. Art says what words can't reach. Gentle movement allows the body to finish emotions the mind keeps looping. Even small rituals matter. *Light a candle. Speak one true sentence aloud in private.* Your nervous system hears that you're ready as it understands ceremony.

This work isn't about becoming a saint or erasing difficult emotions. It's about becoming honest. The aim isn't to delete fear or sadness but to integrate them, so they can sit at the table without running the meeting. Happiness can sit there too. So can grief. Strength can sit beside vulnerability without picking a fight. Hope can keep its voice while uncertainty clears its throat. When parts of you that once lived at war begin to cooperate, you feel it. The noise drops. The room gets bigger.

Presence isn't a forced march into the deepest cave on day one. It's a series of short visits with an exit plan. You touch the feeling, learn one thing, then step back and recover. Over time, you can stay longer without flooding and you need fewer escapes. That isn't weakness. That's wisdom. Go gently and you will go further.

By staying present with your shadows, you do more than endure. You complete yourself. Threads that once sat apart begin to weave into something stronger. You learn that happiness can walk with sorrow, that hope can speak while doubt clears its throat, and that courage often feels less like a drum solo and more like a steady breath.

You might worry that turning toward the shadow will swallow you. In my experience, the opposite is true, as what we run from grows teeth and what we face usually shrinks to size. And sometimes, the wound has more layers than self-help can hold, that's when professional support is needed and contrary to popular belief that isn't failure, it's good judgement. You can't change what you refuse to acknowledge.

Freedom starts to look less like running toward a new life and more like walking with your whole life, one step at a time, head level, eyes open. The dark will always have opinions. Let it talk. Then pick up your lantern and keep moving. You're not running anymore, you're meeting yourself.

If you want a sentence to carry this week, use this one, *'I meet what is here, and I stay kind.'* Say it in the car, at the sink, in the waiting room. It's both a permission slip and a promise. You're not agreeing to fix everything today, you're agreeing not to abandon yourself when things get uncomfortable.

27

I–Me–You–We

Be the person who helps other people's nervous systems think.

THE LONE-WOLF MYTH IS ROMANTIC until the world shows up with people in it. Then *just me* stops working, because your nervous system is a social instrument whether you like it or not. It tunes itself in company.

That's not sentiment, it's wiring, for in attuned, trusting relationships we regulate each other in real time. Breath steadies, tone softens, judgement improves, you're still an individual, but you're also connected to the person across from you, and when it's healthy, to a small *we* that keeps you honest. A life with *Growth* learns that rhythm and plays it on purpose.

I is the channel you broadcast on, when you're attuned, your face, voice, timing, and attention line up with the person in front of you. Their system reads those signals and mirrors them back. Yours mirrors theirs, call it mirror-neuron shorthand if you like, the effect is simple. Two bodies decide, *safe enough, we can think here.* Empathy grows in that climate, not out of thin air. We're more likely to feel into someone when they're familiar, when the situation is vivid, when we've walked a similar road, or when the issue actually matters to us. That's why you can be deeply compassionate with a stranger at work and oddly clumsy at home. Context counts. The fix isn't a bigger performance of care, it's slowing down enough to really see the person you're with, their pace, their language, the thing behind their words they're trying to protect. *Attunement* is accuracy, not acting.

There's a trap here, people confuse attunement with agreement. You don't have to swallow someone's beliefs to tune to their humanity. You pause together long enough for both nervous systems to come back online. Once the alarms settle, disagreement becomes bearable and sometimes useful. Without that pause, it's just two sirens competing for airtime.

<u>Me</u> is the engine room. It's you knowing who's driving the car today, ideally the adult with a plan. Insight isn't the story you've sold yourself, it's the audit, facts over fiction. What actually happened. How it shaped you. What you do under pressure. The values you keep even when they cost. Write your past, present, and future in plain language. No heroics. No self-hatred. The real events and the habits you built to survive them, the patterns that still pay off and the ones that quietly drain you. The person you're practicing being with behaviours, not slogans.

When you untangle biography from mythology, your choices change, you stop expecting the room to treat your history like sacred text and start behaving in ways that earn trust now. That matters because my map is not your map, we don't share a brain, we share a postcode and an intention. When you can name your own glitches, *'I go sideways when plans change. I hear criticism where there's only feedback. Raised voices read as danger in my body,'* you give the people who love you something workable. That isn't weakness. It's handing your team the manual.

<u>You</u> is the bridge. Empathy isn't mind-reading, it's the willingness to be changed by someone else's reality. You don't need to feel what they feel to respect it, you do need to allow that their interpretation makes sense in their body, even if it feels foreign in yours. Awareness asks for that humility, let another person's map exist without repainting it in your colours.

There's a boundary most people skip, you are not a sponge and you can feel with someone without drowning for them. Hold your shape, offer what you can carry. If you flood, you become another problem in the room. That's not kindness, that's leakage.

<u>We</u> is the commons. It's how we behave when no one's clapping, as morality isn't grand statements. It's small, repeatable choices that keep a community dignified. You return the trolley, you speak up, kindly and firmly, when

someone's being steamrolled. You do the right thing on the quiet, because that's who you are, not because there's a camera.

Belonging grows where *we* has rules you can see and trust. Fairness isn't reserved for favourites, status doesn't buy exemptions, quiet voices get airtime, repairs happen quickly and apologies mean something. You can feel your system relax in rooms like that. You also think better. That's the quiet truth. Morality isn't just virtue, it's cognitive hygiene. A fair room gives everyone more usable attention.

Trust is the loop that binds it all. When someone extends trust cleanly, small, specific, no strings, the person trusted often becomes more trustworthy. That's chemistry and dignity working together. Start small, offer an inch you can afford to lose. If it's honoured, offer another. If it's abused, install a fence without a speech. *We* survives when generosity and boundaries share the same table.

The temptation is to turn all this into performance, don't, it's maintenance. You keep the channels clear so people can stay human in the same room. You'll blow it. Everyone does. The win is the repair, *'I spoke sharp. I'm off my game. Let me try that again.'* Repairs thicken trust faster than days where nothing went wrong.

If you want one line to carry into the week, try this, *'Be someone who helps other people's nervous systems think.'* That's what *I, Me, You, We,* comes down to. Do it quietly, do it softly, do it often, it won't trend anywhere, but your home, your work. Your own pulse will tell you you're on the right track. And that's the point, *Growth* doesn't end in isolation or noise, it ends in steadiness, in rooms where people breathe easier because you're there, in a life that feels joined up and worth showing up for again tomorrow.

28

The Quiet Power Of Privacy

In that quiet space, you may just discover the most authentic, peaceful, and powerful version of yourself yet.

IN A WORLD THAT LIVES ON THE LOUDSPEAKER, choosing privacy can feel like swimming upstream. Privacy is power in a world that overshares weakness, where everyone is posting, explaining, defending, and asking for a verdict. Let me say this cleanly. You do not owe anyone access to your inner rooms. Your life will often feel markedly better when fewer people know anything about it, not because you are hiding, but because you are protecting something sacred, your sense of self.

Privacy is not secrecy. Secrecy says, keep this because it is shameful or dangerous. Privacy says, keep this because it is precious. When fewer eyes are on your choices, you stop performing for an audience that never bought tickets and you regain the freedom to change your mind, to start over, to experiment, to fail quietly and try again without commentary. You stop being a character in other people's stories and return to being the author of your own.

Think about how often you have been boxed in by someone else's memory of you. They met a past edition and never downloaded the update, or they project their fears onto your path and call it wisdom. When your life is open to scrutiny, your identity becomes public property, and suddenly you are curating a version of yourself that offends the fewest people. That pressure looks harmless on the surface, however, underneath it breeds anxiety, second-guessing, and emotional fatigue. Privacy enables you to evolve quietly and properly, at your own pace, with fewer hands on the steering wheel.

Some of the strongest work you will ever do happens off camera. Grief that finally moves. A habit that quietly breaks. A course correction that saves your future self years of trouble. No applause. No announcement. Just a person choosing to be decent in private. The internet cannot celebrate that, which is fine, it was never invited. Privacy gives you the silence required for depth so you can hear your own voice again, and you can finally tell the difference between intuition and noise swallowed at speed.

This is not a call to isolation. Keep your people, you tribe, as you still need one or two humans you trust with the unvarnished version of you, a partner, a mate, a Counsellor, someone who knows your first name and your worst day. A confidant who listens like an adult, not a gossip columnist. Share in those spaces, where repair is possible and agendas are small. What you are retiring is the reflex to explain yourself to the crowd. A simple line will do the job. *This is personal right now.* No essay required.

In practical terms, privacy starts with attention, as every time you step into public commentary, you enter a system designed to turn your moments into content. Decide which parts of your life are not available for public consumption. New ideas. Fresh grief. Early recovery. Early romance. Health matters. Creative drafts. Keep early things under shelter and don't publish seedlings and then wonder why the wind took them.

You don't need to over-explain your fences, as a boundary is not a debate club. If someone asks why you are not sharing, try this. *I am keeping this for myself for a while.* That is a complete sentence. Your nervous system will recognise it as safety, and if someone keeps pushing, you have learned something useful about them without having to analyse it further.

Create a few sacred places where your life can sit without judgement. A plain notebook remains one of the cheapest pieces of mental health infrastructure available, as is a short walk where the phone stays home, or a ritual that marks off your time, tea, breath, prayer, candle. These are small practices, however they are also the difference between an inner life that is scattered and one that is steady.

Ask yourself what privacy means for you. Which parts of your life feel calmer when they remain unspoken? Which parts need protection rather than exposure?

The answers will shift with seasons. Moving into *Growth* often requires more shelter, so does fresh grief, early healing, new love, and new ideas. Later, when roots have taken, you can choose what to share, not for validation, but for connection.

There is a common fear that privacy equals smallness and that if you don't announce it, it didn't happen. That is advertising logic, not human logic, as in reality, when you stop crowdsourcing your life, it often becomes larger. Your work improves because you are working, not performing, your relationships deepen because you are present, not narrating the moment for an invisible audience and your mood steadies because you are no longer living inside a permanent talent show.

Privacy also lowers threat in the body. Constant exposure keeps status, certainty, and fairness up for auction. Protect your chemistry as fewer opinions in means fewer spikes out. You'll notice your mind clears when it is no longer rehearsing closing arguments. You may also notice people relax around you when you stop turning every conversation into a panel discussion.

There is a quiet discipline in not posting. When something good happens, let it live in your chest for a while before turning it into content. Share it with a person, not a platform. When something hard happens, wait until you can speak without bleeding on everyone. Then choose your audience deliberately, not because you are fragile, but because you are responsible for the effect your words have on your own system.

If you have lived publicly for a long time, expect some withdrawal, for at fist silence can feel like absence. The itch to prove you are doing okay may intensify, sit with it. That itch is not a command to post, it is a cue to breathe, ground, and reach for a real human. Over time, a different weight arrives, a good one, the feeling that your own life is enough again.

There will be pressure to overshare in the name of authenticity. Authentic does not mean exposed, it means true. Sometimes truth is a full story shared with someone you trust. Sometimes it is a polite on the surface and a real conversation later in the kitchen. You are allowed to finish a chapter before you pass it around.

Privacy creates better decisions. Without an audience, you can choose what is useful over what is impressive. You can step back from plans that looked good in the group chat but feel wrong in your body. You can say no without a speech and yes without a performance. You can pivot without issuing a press release.

There is humour in this too, and you do not need to become a monk or delete the internet. Keep a quiet grin and let people wonder, let them guess. You are busy living, and little a mystery will save you from arguments you never needed to have.

If you want a simple way to begin, try this for one week. First, choose three areas of your life that are off platform and off panel. Second, practice one plain sentence that protects your peace. Third, build one small sanctuary into your day where your mind can land without judgement. Ten minutes is enough. Tea. Pen. Sky. Notice how your shoulders drop. Notice how your thinking sharpens. Notice how courage returns when it no longer has to perform.

Privacy will not make you invincible, however it will make you honest to your self. It will allow your life to grow roots that are not at the mercy of passing weather. It will protect what is early and tender and it will keep your dignity intact when others are careless. It will give you somewhere to stand while you become who you are learning to be.

Live your truth quietly and share when it serves connection, not anxiety. Keep some good things just for you, not because the world is bad, but because your inner world matters. In that quieter space, away from noise and compulsory applause, you may finally meet the version of yourself that has been in waiting for years. Steady. Peaceful. Capable. Keep that person close, and let the rest of the world make do with less.

29

The Unique Strength In Others

Your connections get richer because you are no longer playing against ghosts.

IT CAN START TO FEEL LIKE PEOPLE BLUR into one pattern, especially if you've been let down a few times. Unreliable. Careless. Same old story. The mind gets tired and tries to save energy by slapping on a label and moving on. Then someone steps forward with integrity and a decent heart, and the easy categories wobble. That moment matters. It reminds you that every journey is particular, and that character often shows itself in small details.

Look for the quiet signals. The steady eye contact when someone else is speaking, not the intense stare of a salesman, just the relaxed kind that says, *'I'm here.'* The unhurried respect they give a stranger, not performative, just normal decency with no audience. The way a person owns a mistake without a legal brief. That steadiness is a signpost, it usually means there's been work done inside that you can't see yet, and it leaks out through tone and timing.

Not all teaching arrives with fireworks, often the best education is a plain act of kindness without fanfare. A neighbour who offers a lift and doesn't turn it into a saga. A message that lands at the right minute with no advice attached, just a line that says, *'I'm here.'* A question that invites truth instead of a cross-examination. You can feel the difference. Presence beats performance every time. Copy that part in your own life, listen with real curiosity and follow through on promises without issuing certificates. Decent behaviour doesn't trend, but it builds rooms people want to stay in.

Past experiences will try to write your future for you. The mind loves shortcuts, so it groups people by resemblance and calls it wisdom. *He's like my ex. She's like that boss from 2012. They're all the same.* Once that script starts running, you miss the exceptions that could set you free. When someone behaves against your expectation, don't brush it aside, let it count. If a person takes responsibility instead of dodging, update the file. If they show up when you expected them to disappear, notice it. You don't need to abandon caution, but you do need to notice reality when it changes, otherwise you're fighting ghosts and real people keep paying for crimes they didn't commit.

There's a simple way to challenge your own judgement. Catch the broad statement forming in your head and pause, ask for three pieces of evidence that don't fit the statement. If you can't find any, keep your guard, if you can, loosen the story a notch and keep watching. Character is a pattern over time, not a single scene as much as one good deed doesn't make a saint, one bad day doesn't make a villain. Patterns tell the truth if you give them time.

Everyone carries a private map of setbacks and small victories, no two look the same. What appears to be an overnight rise usually sits on years of unseen routines, self-care, hard conversations, mentors who told the truth when it stung, small efforts that never made it online. When you spot someone ascending, resist the urge to idolise or cut them down, study the elements of their approach and take what fits. Maybe it's their boundaries, maybe it's how they mark progress quietly, maybe it's their habit of asking for help early. You're not copying their life, you're respecting a principle.

There's also skill in giving people time to reveal themselves. Some strengths are quiet on day one as reliability isn't loud and loyalty doesn't announce itself, you find them when the work is dull and they still turn up. Curiosity doesn't swagger, it asks one more question, then listens. Courage isn't always a speech, sometimes it's a clean apology followed by changed behaviour. Watch for these moments, they tell you more than resumes ever will.

If trust has been broken before, a reflex to keep distance will show up, that's ok. Remember, that reflex kept you safe once, so thank it, then refine it. Use boundaries, not barbed wire, for they are conditions for connection. *'I'll meet for coffee, not at midnight. I'll talk tomorrow, not when I'm fried. I'll listen, but I won't be shouted at.'* You'll learn faster with a steady nervous system than with a permanent flinch.

There's a mirror here too. The strengths you admire in others are clues to what you value and need to practice. If you respect someone's calm, notice where your own tone spikes and what would lower it slightly. If you admire follow-through, make one promise this week and keep it. If kindness moves you, look for one plain way to be useful without an invoice attached. You start seeing *Growth* because you're building it, and you build it better because you're seeing it.

Look for the human under the headline. You'll meet people who've done things they regret. If they're doing the work of repair, don't freeze them in the frame of their worst day. Ask what would prove *Growth* here. Fewer excuses. More amends. Consistency under pressure. If those signals appear, let your stance evolve, as holding room for change isn't naïve, it's disciplined hope.

Ground it in real scenes. Someone in a meeting could score points by showing off but instead asks a junior for their view and listens. A friend owns a misstep without padding it with reasons and tells you how they'll handle it next time. A neighbour quietly brings in bins for an older couple with no audience. It looks small. It isn't, for when you bring your awareness to the fore and file those acts under *respect* and your feel your shoulders drop, because your world just got safer. If cynicism has been living in your chest for a while, start gently. Slow the story you tell yourself about people. Watch their behaviour over time and let reality update your view. Make room for exceptions that earn their way in. Offer grace when someone falters, then watch the pattern that follows. Stay curious. Give people the dignity of revealing themselves in their own timeline. When you remember that they're not all the same, you free yourself as much as you free them. Your connections deepen because you're no longer shadowboxing the past. Your compassion grows because you see how hard-won many strengths are. Your own character steadies because you practice the very things you admire, presence, reliability, humility, and kindness and trust.

Meet new people with open curiosity of interest instead of automatic suspicion. Keep your fences but lose the barbs. Let one person at a time surprise you by being better than your fear predicted. If they prove your fear right, you'll know what to do. If they prove it wrong, you'll have made room for something rare and valuable, the unique strength of another human, allowed to stand up in daylight.

30

The Power Of Patience And Observation

Trust that authentic relationships require authenticity from both sides.

RELATIONSHIPS CAN RATTLE YOU, especially when you're unsure about someone's intentions. You've met people who looked like safe harbour and turn into a storm at weeks end, and that kind of swing can shake your confidence and make you doubt your judgement. Here's the steadier truth, everyone shows you who they are if you give them time, and your job isn't to solve them on sight, it's to watch, wait, and let patterns do the talking, for patience sharpens judgment when haste blurs it.

Early on, most people show you a curated version of themselves. It's not always deceit, it's usually just human, because we all want to be accepted and we lead with what we're proud of while we tuck the rest behind a polite smile. That's why first impressions can feel bright and thin at the same time, they're the trailer, not the film. Time is the filter, and life does the testing for you through stress, conflict, fatigue, success, boredom, and disappointment. Those are the scenes that pull the real person into view, and you'll see it in how they handle small power, how they treat someone who can't repay them, and whether they can admit fault without turning it into a courtroom.

Patience is your quiet advantage because it keeps you from rushing in too early or cancelling. You don't need to interrogate, you don't need to play detective, you just observe consistently and let reality stack up. People are a pattern over time, not a moment in neon, and while promises can sound lovely, patterns are proof.

So what do you watch for? Well, in plain terms, watch how they handle disappointment, because anyone can be charming when the tide is in, but character shows when the tide goes out. Do they sulk, blame, ghost, attack, or do they breathe, own their piece, and repair? Watch how they carry stress, because stress doesn't create a new personality, it reveals the one that's been sitting under the surface. Do they turn their upset into your problem, or do they name it and steady themselves without splashing it everywhere? Watch money, time, and truth, because these three don't lie for long. Do they pay what they owe? Do they arrive when they said? Do they tell the truth when it costs? Also watch how they speak about absent people. Today's gossip about others is tomorrow's gossip about you, and you don't want to build trust with someone who treats trust like a hobby.

There are green flags too, and they're rarely flashy. Warmth without performance. Curiosity that asks and then actually listens. Boundaries said calmly and kept quietly. A clean apology followed by changed behaviour, not a dramatic speech followed by the same old nonsense. Small courtesies repeated without an audience. None of this goes viral, and all of it builds *Growth* you can live with.

Patience doesn't mean tolerating harm, because you're not a training ground for someone else's contempt, you can be patient and decisive at the same time. Keep your boundaries close while you observe, and treat a few things as instant deal breakers. No yelling. No threats. No lies. No double life. No secret rules that isolate you from other supports. If one of those shows up, you don't need more data, you more need distance, and you don't need to justify it with a thesis.

Observation works best when you include yourself in the frame. When uncertainty spikes, your mind wants certainty at any price, so slow the rush to decide and give yourself a deep breath, slow exhale, so the thinking part of your brain can rejoin the meeting. Breathe. Shoulders down. Jaw soft. Then ask questions that keep you honest. *'What did I actually see?'* and *'What boundary would make this safe enough to continue?'*

A small private ledger helps, not a dossier, just a note that stops your memory from editing the story later. A few lines after key interactions, *What happened, how you felt, what they did when it was hard.* Patterns need a place to stand, and your future self will thank you for the receipts.

Talk it through with one steady person who knows how to listen, not the mate who pours petrol on everything for entertainment. Say what you've observed and ask what you might be missing, because judgement gets cleaner in company that doesn't need drama to feel alive.

Give it seasons. You don't need to decide the whole relationship in week two. The first phase is the hello, light, pleasant, low stakes, and you're checking whether their words match their behaviour. The second phase is the everyday, where tiredness shows up and plans change and you watch for repair. The third phase is pressure, where life delivers a conflict or a setback, and how they move there tells you more than six perfect dinners ever will.

Be fair about projection as well. Old pain can paint a new person in yesterday's colours, so when a feeling spikes bigger than the scene, name it. *'I'm flooded. This reminds me of 2016.'* Then return to the present and ask, *'What's actually happening here?'* Patience gives you room to separate the past from the person in front of you, and that one skill saves a lot of good connections from being sacrificed to old alarms.

Mind your body while you watch theirs. Your system is an early warning device, so pay attention to tight chest, shallow breath, and that stomach-hardening feeling when a certain topic appears. Don't ignore it, but don't worship it either. Stay curious, because sometimes your brain is spotting a real mismatch, and sometimes it's echoing an old pattern, and time is what helps you tell the difference.

You can learn a lot from small domestic scenes. *How they treat a waiter. Whether they put their phone down when you're speaking. If they soften their tone when you've had a rough day. How they respond to the word no. Whether they keep a promise that isn't convenient.* Quiet behaviour predicts the future louder than grand gestures do.

A note on hope, because observation isn't cynicism, you're not waiting for people to fail, you're giving trust a fair runway and letting truth do the heavy lifting. When someone shows good character over time, let it count, loosen the guard a notch, and offer more of yourself. Connection needs risk, it just doesn't need blind risk. And if the pattern lands poorly, you're still fine, as you've learnt faster and with less damage because you didn't rush, and you can step back with dignity without a courtroom speech. Thank yourself for watching carefully, adjust your filters, and try again when you're ready.

A few practical rules help, especially early. Keep first meetings short and in daylight. Keep early disclosures light and let consistency earn depth. If they pressure you to accelerate intimacy, name your pace and keep it, because people who respect you will respect your tempo, and people who won't are doing you a favour by telling you early. Your nervous system loves your own clarity, and it calms down when you give it a plan. If you want a simple script for the next month, try this. First, *write three non negotiables that keep you safe*. Second, *write three green flags you want to see*. Third, *when you feel pulled to decide fast, read the lists out loud, then wait a day*, because urgency is often just anxiety in a suit.

Bring humour where you can. Relationships are a human sport, you'll misread signals, they'll say the wrong thing, you'll both get tired and ordinary, and that's fine. You're not testing for perfection, you're testing for repair, respect, and repeatable kindness, and if those are present you can carry a lot together. Most of all, extend the same patience to yourself that you're learning to extend to others. You'll miss a red flag. You'll distrust a green flag because your history is loud. Alright. Notice sooner, return to observation, keep your boundaries intact, keep your dignity, and keep moving.

People reveal themselves, it always happens. Let time do its job and let actions speak louder than trailers. When you live this way, you avoid a lot of avoidable pain, and you start building relationships with people who are consistent, trustworthy, and present. That isn't luck. That's patience doing excellent work in the background while you stay steady in the foreground.

Trust that real connection requires authenticity from both sides. Yours shows up as calm clarity and decent boundaries. Theirs shows up as reliable behaviour that matches their words. Give it time. Let the truth surface. Then choose with clear eyes and a settled chest, because that's the strength of patience and observation, it's quiet, it's strong, and it keeps your heart open while your feet stay on solid ground.

131

31

Kindness

Accept that kindness will sometimes be offered to people who don't notice.

UNCONDITIONAL LOVING-KINDNESS SOUNDS SOFT until you actually try to live it. Then you discover it's one of the hardest disciplines going. Not because it's complicated, but because it asks you to give without keeping a ledger, to act decently without applause, and to do good without turning it into a transaction. No receipts. No follow-up. No quiet expectation that the Universe will notice and pay you back.

The point is, doing something kind simply because it's the right thing to do does something subtle and powerful inside you. It builds self-respect, not the noisy kind, the grounded kind. The kind that lets you sleep better and walk through the day with your shoulders a little lower. Kindness given freely doesn't drain you, it steadies you, it reminds you who you are when nobody's watching.

Let's clear up a common confusion. Loving-kindness is not people-pleasing, for that's fear with a smile on as it says yes when it should say no, then resents the person it never told the truth to. Loving-kindness has a spine, it knows its limits, it offers what it can give cleanly and stops there. If your kindness leaves you bitter, exhausted, or quietly angry because of what wasn't recognised, it wasn't kindness, it was self-aggrandisement.

Start at home, and I don't mean your house, I mean your inner world. The tone you use with yourself sets the ceiling for the kindness you can offer others. If your inner voice is a drill sergeant or a courtroom prosecutor, generosity will always feel forced. Speak to yourself like someone you're responsible for, clear, decent, practical. Eat, rest, step outside. Self-kindness isn't indulgence, it's maintenance. Try again.

Outwardly, the most effective loving-kindness to others is specific and small. Big gestures are easy to admire and hard to sustain, whilst small, repeatable acts change climates. Thank someone by naming what they actually did, hold a door without performing it, put the trolley back, let someone merge, answer the email you could ignore. These aren't moral heroics, they're social hygiene and they make shared spaces easier to breathe in.

Kindness also knows when to be quiet. Not every problem needs your advice, sometimes the kindest move is to listen without fixing, to sit in the discomfort without trying to tidy it up. Ask once, *'Do you want help or do you want company?'* Then respect the answer. Presence, real presence, is rarer than solutions and often far more healing.

In conflict, loving-kindness looks like restraint. You don't go for the throat even when you know where it is, you speak about behaviour, not character. You don't unload on a collegue for past offences to win the moment, you say what needs to be said in a way that leaves the door open for repair. That isn't weakness, that's emotional strength under control.

Boundaries belong here too. A clear boundary is an act of loving-kindness to both sides as it prevents confusion, resentment, and quiet scorekeeping. *'I'm available after seven. I won't be spoken to like that.'* Say it calmly and mean it. People who respect you will adjust, people who don't were never responding to kindness anyway, only access.

There's also loving-kindness that lives in systems. You make things easier for the next person without being asked. You label, you document, you tidy, you close loops, you design your life and work so fewer people need rescuing. That's loving-kindness with foresight, it saves a tonne of energy, including your own.

Online, loving-kindness means not feeding the outrage machine. You don't pile on, you don't perform righteousness for strangers. You praise in private. You step away when you're heated. You remember there's a human nervous system on the other side of the screen, even when they've forgotten it themselves. You don't have to win every point to keep your dignity.

In families, loving-kindness shows up as consistency. You greet properly, you apologise when you miss, you repair quickly, you don't weaponise silence, you don't keep score and you show your kids and your partner what accountability looks like in real time. That's how safety is built, not by perfection, but by reliable repair.

If you're caring for someone in pain, loving-kindness gets very practical. You offer two options, not an open-ended promise, you show up when you said you would, you leave when you said you would, you don't try to explain their pain away you help carry it, then you come back tomorrow. That steadiness matters more than words.

Some loving-kindness will land nowhere. It won't be noticed, it won't be returned, it might even be misunderstood. Do it anyway. Not because you're hoping for cosmic credit, but because your nervous system is always watching your own behaviour.

If you want a simple practice, keep it this small. One unrequested, unadvertised act of loving-kindness a day. Something that costs little and means something. Don't post it, don't explain it, let it belong to you. Over time, this changes how you move through the world. You become less reactive, less transactional, more grounded. This *Growth* doesn't arrive with fireworks, but quietly, as a sense that you're living in alignment.

So pick one thing today. Send the message, hold the line kindly, clean up something that wasn't your mess, speak to yourself with respect, then get on with your life. That's unconditional loving-kindness, ordinary, repeatable, and far more powerful than it looks.

32

Relationships Matter

The rest of life gets lighter when you stop dragging your relationships behind you.

BY FAR THE GREATEST PREDICTOR OF HAPPINESS is not achievement, comfort, or getting life right, it is the quality of your relationships, with family, friends, community, and just as importantly, with yourself. Because long after status fades and circumstances shift, it is connection that keeps people steady, sane, and meaningfully alive.

Study after study confirms what lived experience already knows, people who feel securely connected suffer less, recover faster, and live longer, not because life treats them more gently, but because they don't face it alone.

This is not about popularity or social noise, and it certainly isn't about curating a crowd. It is about depth over breadth, about having a small number of relationships where you are known, accepted, and able to be honest, and about developing a relationship with yourself that does not collapse into contempt the moment you fall short. Happiness grows where belonging is real, and belonging begins inside.

The first relationship to examine, uncomfortable as it may be, is the one you have with yourself. The tone of your inner dialogue quietly shapes every other connection in your life, because if you speak to yourself with constant criticism, impatience, or ridicule, you will either tolerate poor treatment from others or keep them at a safe distance to avoid confirming what you already fear. The standard you live with internally becomes the standard you accept externally.

Learning to speak to yourself with firmness and fairness, without cruelty or indulgence, is not self-love theatre, it is self-respect, and it lays the groundwork for healthier choices in every other relationship you form.

Relationships themselves are not built on intentions or promises, they are built on patterns, on what people do consistently when no one is watching, when things are inconvenient, or when emotions are running high. Anyone can be warm in the early days or generous when the cost is low, but character reveals itself in how someone responds to boundaries, how they speak about people who are absent, how they behave when plans change or success arrives unevenly.

Charm may open a door, but character determines whether it stays open.

Many people have been hurt not because they trusted too deeply, but because they trusted too quickly, mistaking intensity for intimacy and familiarity for safety. Early connection can feel like oxygen after a long drought, and that feeling is real, but it is not yet evidence. Time is the only reliable filter. Over months and seasons you learn how someone repairs, how they manage frustration, how they carry responsibility, and whether their values hold under pressure. Letting time do its work is not pessimism, it's wisdom.

Boundaries are the companion to patience, and they are often misunderstood. They are not punishments or ultimatums, they are conditions for dignity, spoken plainly and enforced calmly. *'I can talk later, not now. I won't accept that tone. I'm available here, not there.'* Boundaries do not require justification or emotional padding, because clarity is kinder than confusion. People who respect you will adapt, and people who rely on your compliance will protest, but peace built on self-betrayal is always short-lived and expensive.

No relationship survives without repair. Hurt is inevitable wherever humans gather, so the defining feature of a healthy connection is not the absence of conflict, but the speed, honesty, and cleanliness of repair. Learning to say, *'That's on me,'* without defending yourself, and learning to hear, *'That hurt,'* without preparing a counter-argument, keeps relationships from calcifying into resentment. Repairs done early thicken trust, while repairs delayed often arrive too late to matter.

Not every disagreement needs an audience, and not every emotional process belongs in the group chat. Keeping the tender parts of your relationships contained within appropriate walls is not secrecy, it is stewardship. When you protect someone's dignity when they are not present, you signal that you are safe to be close to, and that trust is not something you spend lightly.

Disagreement, when handled well, can deepen connection rather than erode it. The key is staying focused on behaviour rather than character, on the present moment rather than a catalogue of past grievances, and on solutions rather than victories.

Generosity sustains relationships when it is freely given, not when it is tracked. Keeping a hidden ledger of who owes whom quietly poisons connection, turning kindness into leverage and affection into currency. At the same time, generosity without boundaries becomes resentment in waiting, so the aim is balance, giving what you can carry without bitterness and stopping before self-sacrifice becomes self-erasure.

Affection, often overlooked, is one of the simplest and most powerful relational nutrients. A genuine greeting, a brief message of care, a moment of undivided attention, these small gestures accumulate, forming the mortar that holds relationships together over time. Most relationships do not fail because of one dramatic betrayal, they fade because warmth slowly leaves the room.

Friendships, like any living thing, require maintenance. Nostalgia is not a substitute for presence, and distance does not end friendships as reliably as neglect does. Small, consistent gestures of contact, a message, a call, a shared walk, remind people that they matter. Some friendships are seasonal and letting them end without bitterness is a sign of maturity, not failure.

Workplace relationships benefit from clear roles and respectful limits. Civility, reliability, and fairness go further than forced intimacy ever will. Leaders who communicate expectations clearly, give feedback early, and keep their word create environments where people feel safe enough to do good work. Respect grows where rules are visible and applied consistently.

Family relationships are often the most complex, shaped by inherited roles and unspoken rules that may no longer fit the adults we've become. Loving someone does not require unlimited access, and updating boundaries is not betrayal, it is

Growth. You are allowed to keep what nourishes you and decline what costs you your peace.

Romantic relationships flourish when friendship is treated as foundational rather than optional. Curiosity, clear communication, repair, humour, and respect for each other's individuality matter more over time than chemistry alone. Choosing someone you can be ordinary with, someone who repairs rather than performs, is often the difference between lasting connection and chronic exhaustion.

Past hurt can make caution sensible, but turning caution into a fortress eventually costs you intimacy. Fences work better than walls, allowing you to see clearly, control access, and adjust as evidence accumulates. Accuracy, not numbness, is the goal. When crisis arrives, as it inevitably does, relationships reveal their true health. Who shows up, who disappears, and who offers practical presence without spectacle becomes clear. Remember quietly. Return care when you can. This is how trust compounds over time.

Humour, used gently, keeps relationships flexible. Sarcasm corrodes, while kindness paired with wit releases tension without costing dignity. Laughing together at life's absurdities makes room for grace when things get heavy.

Rituals carry relationships through emotional low tides. Regular check-ins, predictable moments together, and shared routines provide continuity when feelings fluctuate, because feelings always do. Rhythm outlasts intensity.

Fatigue turns good people into brittle versions of themselves, so sleep, nourishment, movement, and the courage to say no are not luxuries, they are prerequisites for staying kind. You are not fragile, but you are finite, and pretending otherwise is how relationships fray.

You don't need perfect relationships to achieve *Growth* in life. You need honest ones, built with patience, protected by boundaries, repaired without drama, and warmed by everyday acts of care. When relationships are nurtured this way, life becomes lighter to carry, not because it hurts less, but because you are no longer carrying it alone.

33

The Write Way

Life will remain life, messy, beautiful, occasionally unforgiving.

THE DAY IS NOISY AND FORGETFUL, and if you don't keep a record, the loudest moment wins, which is rarely the wisest or the most representative.

Journaling is how you stop letting your worst five minutes narrate your entire life. It isn't a diary of moods unless that genuinely serves you. It's a ledger of reality, what worked, what didn't, and what you'll try next, less confession and more captain's log, written by someone who intends to keep the ship afloat.

Start by making it boring enough to survive contact with real life, because the enemy of a journal is ambition. If you insist on candlelight, perfect insights, and a minimum word count, you'll write twice and quit. Strip it back to what repeats. Same time each day, same place, same short shape. Two to five sentences will do. One thing that went well. One thing you'll do tomorrow. One line of context if it helps. That's enough to catch the drift of your life without turning the practice into theatre.

Facts come first. *'Called Mum when I didn't feel like it. Walked eighteen minutes. Asked a clean question in the meeting and saved three hours of confusion.'* Then add one line of analysis, why did this work? Then one line of instruction for repair. This is how you train your attention to notice what's repeatable and useful rather than spiralling on what's vague and bad. Over time, your journal becomes a manual written by you, for you, based on evidence instead of hope.

Your journal is also the right place to practice privacy. You don't owe anyone your raw drafts. The value is telling the truth to yourself without performing it for an audience. Privacy gives you room to change your mind, upgrade your behaviour, and experiment without carrying a crowd. In a loud world, that kind of sovereignty is rare and worth protecting.

Patterns matter more than events. After a fortnight, read back and circle recurring words. Sleep. Walks. Boundaries. Screens. Tone. Which actions correlate with steadier mornings? Which choices predict a cleaner night? Your journal will show you the compound interest of plain decisions, the week you went to bed on purpose, the month you put the phone outside the bedroom, the season you stopped defending relationships that drained you. This isn't personality change. It's maintenance.

When the page feels empty, use simple prompts. *What would make today matter? What am I avoiding? What would help by ten per cent? What can I control in the next hour?* These aren't tricks, they're steering wheels. Answer them briefly and honestly and the day becomes navigable by choice rather than weather.

If you've lived through trauma, illness, or long uncertainty, journaling has an extra job. It separates past from present. Write one line that acknowledges the old story, then one line that anchors the now. *Yes, that happened. Today I took my meds, rang the GP, and walked ten minutes.* The brain loves to collapse timelines, your journal refuses to. This is how you stop history from swallowing today whole.

Don't let the journal become a courtroom where you prosecute yourself. The point is to build a trustworthy narrator, not a harsher judge, so when you miss a day, write the next one without apology. No make-up homework as shame is terrible fuel for change. Curiosity works better, *'Interesting that I skipped yesterday. What was I avoiding.'* Ask, learn, move.

From time to time, elevate an entry into a decision by putting a box around it. *'From today, no work email after six. From today, one kindness before lunch.'* Date it. Review those boxes monthly. You're not writing commandments, you're building a constitution, a set of decent defaults that make life easier for the future you.

Consider the physical setup. A cheap note often beats a glowing app because your hand moves at the speed of sense-making. But if an app keeps you consistent, use it. The only rule is repeatability. Keep the tools where the habit lives. Pen with the kettle. Notebook on the bedside. App tile on the home screen. Everything else that distracts you goes to page two and stays there.

Journaling also strengthens relationships. After a difficult conversation, write one short paragraph, *What you heard. What you felt. What boundary you'll hold next time. What you appreciate about the person despite the issue.* This turns conflict from a loop into a ladder. When you meet again, you're not starting from scratch, you have notes. People feel safer around someone who learns.

On good days, use the journal to bank gratitude. On bad days, use it to bank survival. *'Did the minimum today,'* which counts as there will be seasons where the minimum is heroic, it lets the record show that you kept showing up. Those pages will rescue you later, when impostor feelings try to rewrite your history.

You might worry about posterity, what if someone reads this. That's why entries stay short, factual, and decent. Write as if you're the primary reader, because you are, and as if future you will be grateful for the clarity, because they will. If a sentence would humiliate you out of context, refine it to the honest core or don't write it. That isn't censorship. It's self-respect.

Close each day on purpose. One line of thanks. One line of truth. One line of intention. *'Grateful for the rain. Tired and cranky but showed up anyway. Tomorrow, call the accountant at nine.'* Then put the day to bed. You don't need to carry it into the night. Your mind will keep working while you sleep. Give it a clean brief to work on.

Journaling won't save you from difficulty, and it shouldn't. Life will remain life, messy, beautiful, occasionally unforgiving. What this practice gives you is a steady narrator, someone who doesn't dramatise or minimise, who looks at the day, names what happened, and sets the next marker. A steady narrator is worth their weight in gold. Keep one. It will keep you in good stead.

34

Catch the Good While It's Happening

So yes, life is often noisy, prickly, and occasionally absurd, be grateful
anyway.

GRATITUDE ISN'T ABOUT PRETENDING everything's fine while the roof leaks and the dog's chewed your last decent sock. It's not a caption, a posture, or a performance. Done properly, gratitude is a discipline of attention, a way of teaching your mind to register useful good in the wild, not just danger. Think of it as calibrating your internal instruments so they don't scream mayday every time the wind shifts. Life stays messy. You get steadier.

Begin small and stay specific. *'I'm grateful for my family'* is pleasant, but it's too broad to train anything. *'I'm grateful for the way my daughter laughed at breakfast and changed the weather in the kitchen.'* gives your brain a clear target. Specificity is instruction. When you name the detail, the sound of cutlery settling after a joke, the warmth of the first sip of tea, the message that arrived kinder than expected, you're telling your attention, this matters, find more like this tomorrow. You're not writing poetry, you 're writing cues.

After each item, pause and ask the question most people skip, *'Why did this good thing happen?'* The answer often reveals a behaviour you can repeat. *You left five minutes early, you messaged first, you set a boundary, you put the phone face-down, you tackled the ugly email yesterday so this morning was calmer.* Now gratitude turns practical, you're not just thankful, you're reverse-engineering causes. Days improve on purpose rather than by luck.

When you can express gratitude cleanly, do it. A quiet *'Thanks for sorting that.'* does two things at once. It reinforces the behaviour in them and it strengthens the noticing habit in you. Gratitude expressed is social glue, it makes families less prickly, teams less brittle, and strangers less strange. Keep it short and true.

No theatre. You're not auditioning for sainthood, you're marking the moment so it doesn't slip through the cracks.

Gratitude is not denial. On hard days, shrink the frame, trade grand for granular. *'The nurse was gentle. The rain helped the garden. I kept my temper when I didn't want to.'* This small discipline stops the worst five minutes from narrating the whole chapter.

A warning worth hearing. Gratitude can be misused as emotional duct tape, slapped over legitimate pain to make other people comfortable. Don't do that to yourself. Gratitude belongs alongside truth, not instead of it. You can be grateful for the casserole and still furious about the diagnosis. Adults can hold two realities at once.

Savouring is gratitude's close cousin. When a good thing happens, stretch it by ten seconds. Slow the fork before the second bite. Let the warm air on the steps touch your face properly. Notice two details and take one deliberate breath. This isn't indulgence, it's teaching your nervous system to register safety and pleasure so it doesn't spend the whole day scanning for ambushes. Rehearsed happiness is still happiness.

Food is an excellent training ground because it's already there. Slow the fork for one bite per meal. Just one. Actually taste the thing you paid for. Texture, heat, salt, spice. This isn't about indulgence or rules, it's about honesty. If the bite is good, call it good. If it's rubbish, you'll know sooner and stop chasing satisfaction with your face still in the bowl. Savouring sharpens discernment. You become harder to impress and easier to please, which is a very comfortable combination to live with.

Nature helps because it doesn't ask anything of you. Step into it on purpose, even if your version of nature is a scrappy gum tree and a square of sky. Notice the direction of the wind, the colour of the light, the way yesterday's heat still lives in the footpath. This isn't spiritual theatre. It's your nervous system scanning the room and discovering that, for this moment, nothing is attacking you. People who practice this are less rattled by traffic, deadlines, and opinionated relatives because their body remembers there are other states available.

There's a private side to savouring that matters more than most people realise. Keep some moments just for you. If every good thing turns into content, your attention starts hunting angles instead of depth. Take a photo occasionally if it helps you return later, but don't turn your life into a storyboard. Some moments do their best work precisely because no one else knows about them. Protect those. They're building something quiet and sturdy inside you.

At work, build thank-you loops. End an email that went somewhere with a line naming the helpful behaviour. Gratitude up and down the ladder both matter. Over time you normalise noticing contribution rather than just error, and the room gets easier to think in.

Boundaries still apply. Gratitude doesn't mean tolerating nonsense. You can be thankful and firm in the same breath. *'I appreciate the effort here, and we still need the brief next week.'* It lets you be kind without becoming vague.

If you're rebuilding after illness, depression, or a long hard season, start microscopic. Be grateful for the precise place your feet touch the floor. Be grateful you took the tablet you didn't want to take. Be grateful you opened the window. You're not ordering sunshine, you're registering light where it already exists. Some days the list will be one line long, that's enough. Tomorrow you add a second.

At home, gratitude becomes culture. Catch people doing things right and name it in real time. Keep it ordinary. *'Loved how you handled that call. Thanks for making space for quiet.'* People who are noticed for effort and repair learn to notice those things in themselves.

Keep the language plain. Your mind doesn't need lofty phrases. It needs usable cues. *'Today was better because I walked early. Tea and sunlight on the steps. She listened without fixing.'* These notes are easy to reread on grim afternoons when the story in your head goes dark. Clarity is a light switch.

Expect some pushback. The inner critic will sneer that you're being corny. Reply that you're being specific. The cynic will call it soft. Smile and change nothing. Gratitude isn't a personality. It's a practice. In a month you won't be a different person. You'll be a steadier one. The people who live with you will notice first.

Gratitude compounds. A day of noticing does very little. A fortnight redirects attention. A season builds a ledger of decent days, and that ledger changes how you meet trouble. You'll still get blindsided, everyone does, but you won't be empty-handed. You'll have proof that you recover, that there are resources, that there are people.

.

35

You've Got This!

YOU'RE NOT TRYING TO IMPRESS ANYONE, and not everything decent needs a camera, for some moments are yours alone, and keeping them that way protects your sense that life is allowed to be private and meaningful without applause.

So yes, life is noisy, prickly, and occasionally absurd. Be grateful anyway, specifically, privately, repeatedly. Not because everything is fine, but because some things are good and worth naming.

You're becoming someone your future self can rely on, clear-eyed, present, and able to recognise a decent moment when it's standing right in front of you

Quick Recap

Adversity: Asks the real questions. 'Who are you when the plan breaks? What will you hold? What will you put down?'

Affective Forecasting: Predicting tomorrow's feelings with today's mood.

Affect Label: Put the feeling into five plain words. Naming it drops the heat and quietly activates your brakes. That's not poetry, that's wiring.

Allostatic Load: When the accumulated strain of keeping your system braced starts to climb, ready for action, your sleep thins, your patience leaks, your biology is being taxed beyond design.

Amygdala: (Flight, Flight, Freeze) prepares the body to protect itself from a perceived threat without conscious thought.

Attention: Train your internal radar to notice the full scene, not just the sirens. When a decent moment lands, savour it for ten honest seconds. Where your attention goes, your day goes. Ask better questions. Not, *'Why am I like this?'* Try, *'What would help by ten per cent?'*

Attentional Intelligence: The skill of deliberately choosing where your focus goes, instead of letting noise, habit, or emotion decide for you.

Attribution Bias: You had reasons, they have flaws.

Autonomy: The right to steer your own trolley. It's not rebellion, it's oxygen.

Availability Bias: Believing whatever's loudest or latest.

Certainty: Your brain is a prediction machine that prefers any map to none.

Cognitive Dissonance: Ignoring the need to change what you're doing or rewrite the story you tell yourself when there is inconsistency between your knowledge and your behaviour.

Confirmation Bias: Collecting evidence for the story you like.

Congruence: When your goals stop being slogans and start resembling your calendar.

Consistency: When your chemistry and psychology stop fighting and start pulling the same way.

Courage: Isn't a speech, it's doing the next small right thing while your stomach does somersaults.

Chaos toward Coherence: It's not a straight line, it's the slow 'Integration' of your life's parts so they stop pulling against each other.

Counterfactual Thinking: Giving thanks for what 'didn't' happen.

Cortical Firing: Networks that light up together, like streets on a night map, with the prefrontal cortex your air-traffic control, coordinating the lot.

Discomfort: Often the start of a more honest track, the very feeling you're trying to run from is the nudge that says, "Look here, grow here, set a fence here, soften here."

Emotional Brain: Links your emotions to your physical responses, like how stress can raises blood pressure.

Emotional Contagion: Watch it in a café queue, one grumpy bloke infects three people deep upturned smiles, whilst the Barista with a proper smile, flips the chemistry of the room to a positive vibe.

Emotional Regulation: Isn't about being calm all the time, it's about having enough awareness to shift what you feel or how you respond rather than letting old automatic settings run the show.

Expectation Management: If you keep handing your hope to people who have shown you they'll drop it, you'll end up jaded and noisy. Honour reality, believe patterns, not promises.

Fairness is the quiet judge: It doesn't shout until it's been ignored for a while, then it brings the whole tent down.

Flow: That inner state where you're so engaged in an activity that time goes quiet, your thoughts stop tripping over themselves, and you're in your own world in the best possible way.

Frazzle: Like the end of a worn-out rope that is unravelling and weak, negatively impacting your ability to focus, concentrate, and remember multiple things.

Future Forecasting: Tries to feel tomorrow with today's emotions. If you insist on being in the future, congratulations, you're already here, it's called *Now*.

Gratitude: Being aware of and promoting the positive things that occur in your life, and be thankful.

Hardship: Peels away the theatre and shows you where you're strong and where there's work to do, it's unromantic, but it's also liberating.

Happiness: Should be the by-product of *Growth* not the goal.

Hedonic Adaptation: The mind's habit of quickly normalising gains and comforts, which is why chasing 'more' stops working and lasting satisfaction has to be built from how you live, not what you get.

Impartial Spectator: The calm observer who can see you from a slight distance without malice

Implicit Memory: The unconscious, automatic form of memory that allows you to perform tasks and be influenced by past experiences without deliberately thinking about them.

Insight: Doesn't come wrapped in a bow, it knocks on the door after a mess and asks, *'Are you ready to learn something you couldn't learn any other way?'*

Intention: When you show up again and again, especially when it stings, you build small rituals that steady your inner weather, what mattered and why.

Intentional Emotional Regulation: The conscious effort to shift what you feel or how you respond, rather than letting old automatic settings run the show. You're balancing threat and reward in your body and brain, moment by moment, a balance that is never once and done, it's a set of dials you keep adjusting.

Limbic System: Your brain's emotional engine, quickly scanning for threat or safety and driving feelings and reactions long before logic gets a chance to weigh in.

Meaning: Happiness without meaning, it feels like fairy floss, nice, then nothing. Meaning grows when you carry weight that matters and carry it cleanly. It's in being useful to real people, not impressive to imaginary ones.

Metacognition: The process of you becoming aware of and analysing your own thought and learning processes, so you can choose a better response instead of running on autopilot.

Mindful Attention: Builds your ability to set small goals you can actually hit, decent self-talk you put on a repeating loop, when you'd rather throw the Guide across the room.

Mindfulness: The simple, disciplined act of paying attention to what's actually happening right now, without trying to fix it, flee it, or turn it into a story about who you are.

Mirror Neurons: Your nervous system tunes to the room whether you asked it to or not. They light up when you see a face, a posture, a tone. Someone smiles and your circuitry warms, someone flinches and your body readies for impact.

Monkey Mind:, Runs the switchboard, restless, jumpy, half gossip, half weather report. Thoughts swing from limb to limb and back again.

Neuroplasticity: The brain's ability to reorganise its structure, function, and connections throughout life in response to new experiences, learning, or injury.

Noetic: Being aware of your knowing (inner-self), your sentience. Your conscious awareness of self.

Optimism: The steady decision to expect workable outcomes and keep moving toward them, not because life is easy, but because your actions shape what happens next.

Persistence: Isn't perfection, it's staying 'present' with 'what is', and trusting that it's enough to move on with one more clean step.

Prefrontal Cortex: The part of your brain that helps you pause, plan, and choose a response that serves your future rather than reacting on impulse in the moment.

Presence: The invitation to see beauty in small things, comfort in the ordinary, courage in the unresolved and anchoring your awareness in the here and now, including what you would rather avoid.

Privacy and Pace: Not every good thing needs an audience. Keep some victories unadvertised so they can do deep work without being chewed by opinion. Tell a person, not a platform.

Reappraise: Change the meaning of the moment, *'This urge isn't a command it's a wave.'*

Re-entry Loop: The repeating cycle where experience becomes interpretation, interpretation becomes wiring, and wiring steers the interpretation of next experience.

Regulate: The way you repair after a mistake, the way you speak when you're tired, all of it affects the people within your reach. That's not pressure to perform, it's motivation to practice. When you strengthen your inner steadiness, everyone who sits at your table breathes a little easier.

Relatedness: The 'us' button. Your system is forever sorting people into safe, watch, and do not engage without biscuits.

Resilience: Isn't grown on a couch under perfect light, it shows up when the plan falls apart and you have learnt under duress to keep peeling back the blankets and placing one foot after another.

Rumination: The repetitive thinking about either negative past or future experiences or worries.

Savouring and Filing: When something decent happens, register it with all your senses for a few honest seconds. Shelve it properly. You will find it later when the day tries to tell you nothing good ever happens

Self-Awareness: The ability to notice your thoughts, feelings, and behaviours as they happen, so you can choose your next move instead of running on autopilot.

Self-Directed Neuroplasticity: Is you choosing which streets get the new bitumen. Repeat a path with attention and emotion and the map updates.

Sentient Awareness: The basic capacity to know that you are here, alive, and experiencing this moment, before thought, language, or story get involved.

Status: Isn't peacocking, it's the basic question. *'Am I being respected here?'*

Steadiness: That tone the floor of happiness stands on. Aiming for 'just not making it worse', is sometimes the bravest thing you'll do. It's the tone you use at the beginning.

Sunk-Cost Fallacy: Throwing good times after bad because you've already paid.

Malcom C. McCullough

References

Barrett, L. *How Emotions Are Made: The Secret Life of the Brain.*

Bebko, G. et al. *Look before you regulate: Differential perceptual strategies underlying expressive suppression and cognitive reappraisal.*

Berkman. E, Lieberman. *Using Neuroscience to broaden emotion regulation: Theoretical and methodological considerations.*

Bradt, S. *Mind is a frequent, but not happy, wanderer: People spend nearly half their waking hours thinking about what isn't going on around them.*

Braham, A. *Four ways of letting go.*

Chopra, D. *Spiritual Solutions.*

Crawford. J. *The brain friendly organisation: What leadership needs to know for intelligence to flourish.*

Davachi, L. *Learning that lasts through the AGES.*

Davis. J, Gross.J, & Ochsner.K. *Psychological distance and emotional experience: What you see is what you get. Emotion.*

Du Savtoy. D, and Hayne. JD. *Neuroscience and Freewill.*

Eisenberger, N.I. *Social Pain and the Brain.*

Eisenberger, N.I. *Current Directions in Psychological Science.*

Fralich, T. *Mindfulness: Integrating cutting edge neuroscience and mindfulness skills in the treatment of Mental Health disorders and emotional dysregulation.*

Findlay, J. *Change Agility.*

Giddens, A. *Modernity and Self Identity.*

Gilbert, D. *Why we make bad decisions.*

Goldin, P. *The Neuroscience of emotions.*

Gonsalez, V. and Mark, G. *Constant Multitasking Craziness: Managing Multiple Working Spheres.*

Greenleaf, R. *The Servant as a Leader.*

Jones, A. *Business Leaders Agree: Empathy is the single most important skills in business today.*

Kabit-Zinn, J. *Mindfulness For Beginners.*

Kabat-Zinn, J. *Mindfulness for life.*

Kerr, C. *Mindfulness starts with the body: A view from the brain.*

Lieberman. M. *The brain's braking system and how to use your words to tap into it.*

Lieberman, M. Eisenberger. N. *The pains and pleasures of social life: A social cognitive neuroscience approach.*

MacDonald, G. & Leary, M. R. *Why does social exclusion hurt? The relationship between social and physical pain.*

Munday, I. & Kneebone, I. & Rogers, K. & Newton-John, T. *The Language of Pain: Is There a Relationship Between Metaphor Use and Adjustment to Chronic Pain.*

Neal, D. & Wood, W. *The pull of the past: When do habits persist despite conflict with motives.*

Novell, D. *Positive Psychology and the Science of Sustained Happiness.*

Pashler, H. *Attention and Performance.*

Peck, M.S. *The Different Drum.*

Prochaska, J. O. & DiClemente, C. C. *Transtheoretical therapy: Toward a more integrative model of change.*

Ramachandran, V. *How Mirror Neurons Help Us To Learn New Skills And Create Empathy For Others.*

Rameson.L, and Lieberman. L. *Empathy: A Social Cognitive Neuroscience Approach.*

Ray, L. *Attention Matters: What's your self regulation checklist?*

Ray, L. *Attention Matters: Is there an upside to interruption Brainwaves for Leaders.*

Ray, L. *Attention Matters: Working with a mindful brain. Brainwaves for Leaders.*

Rock, D. *Managing with the Brain in Mind.*

Rock, D. *Your brain at work. Strategies for overcoming distraction, regain focus and working smarter all day long.*

Rock, D. & Siegal, D. *The Healthy Mind Platter.*

Schultz, K. *Only if, if Only. (On Being Wrong).*

Schwartz, J., Gaito, P. & Lennicj, D. *That's the way we (used to) do things around here.*

Shiv, B. *Brain Research at Stanford: Decision Making.*

Sheeran. P, Webb. L, & Gollwitzer. P. *The interplay between goal intentions and implementation intentions.*

Siegal, D. *The Mindful Brain: Reflection and Attunement in the cultivation of Well Being.*

Siegal, D. *Brain of the Mindful Therapist.*

Malcom C. McCullough

Siegal, D. *The Neurological Basis of Behaviour, the Mind, the Brain and Human Relationship*.

Siegal, D. *Mindsight. Insight/Empathy/Integration*.

Siegal, D. *Transforming Chaos and Rigidity to Coherence. Mindfulness: Defining the mind and well-being*.

Sousa, D. *Brainwork: The neuroscience behind how we lead others*.

Veneziani, V. *A visual study guide to cognitive biases*.

Zak, P. *The Trust Molecule*.

www.ingramcontent.com/pod-product-compliance
Lightning Source LLC
Chambersburg PA
CBHW032111280326
41933CB00009B/800